Cambridge Topics in English Language

Language and Power

Gary Ives and Raj Rana
Series Editors: Dan Clayton and Marcello Giovanelli

CAMBRIDGE
UNIVERSITY PRESS

University Printing House, Cambridge CB2 8BS, United Kingdom

One Liberty Plaza, 20th Floor, New York, NY 10006, USA

477 Williamstown Road, Port Melbourne, VIC 3207, Australia

314–321, 3rd Floor, Plot 3, Splendor Forum, Jasola District Centre, New Delhi – 110025, India

79 Anson Road, #06–04/06, Singapore 079906

Cambridge University Press is part of the University of Cambridge.

It furthers the University's mission by disseminating knowledge in the pursuit of education, learning and research at the highest international levels of excellence.

www.cambridge.org
Information on this title: www.cambridge.org/9781108402132

© Cambridge University Press 2018

This publication is in copyright. Subject to statutory exception and to the provisions of relevant collective licensing agreements, no reproduction of any part may take place without the written permission of Cambridge University Press.

First published 2018

20 19 18 17 16 15 14 13 12 11 10 9 8 7 6 5 4 3

Printed in Great Britain by CPI Group (UK) Ltd, Croydon CR0 4YY

A catalogue record for this publication is available from the British Library

ISBN 978-1-108-40213-2 Paperback

Cambridge University Press has no responsibility for the persistence or accuracy of URLs for external or third-party internet websites referred to in this publication, and does not guarantee that any content on such websites is, or will remain, accurate or appropriate.

....

NOTICE TO TEACHERS IN THE UK
It is illegal to reproduce any part of this work in material form (including photocopying and electronic storage) except under the following circumstances:
(i) where you are abiding by a licence granted to your school or institution by the Copyright Licensing Agency;
(ii) where no such licence exists, or where you wish to exceed the terms of a licence, and you have gained the written permission of Cambridge University Press;
(iii) where you are allowed to reproduce without permission under the provisions of Chapter 3 of the Copyright, Designs and Patents Act 1988, which covers, for example, the reproduction of short passages within certain types of educational anthology and reproduction for the purposes of setting examination questions.

Contents

Series introduction	v
How to use this book	vi
Topic introduction	vii
1. Language and power	**1**
1.1 Inequality and power imbalance in society	2
1.2 The power of language	6
2. Types of power	**10**
2.1 Concepts about power	11
2.2 Politeness as a power tool	24
2.3 Power and genre	26
3. Language, power and the media	**30**
3.1 Access to the media	31
3.2 The language and power of journalism	32
3.3 The language and power of advertising	40
3.4 The language and power of charity appeals	48
4. Language, power and occupation	**51**
4.1 Exclusive features of occupational language	52
4.2 Workplace interactions	56
4.3 The negotiation of roles: the customer is always right	60
5. Language, power and education	**64**
5.1 Traditional classroom discourse	65
5.2 A more collaborative classroom	71
6. Language, power and politics	**75**
6.1 Ideology and Critical Discourse Analysis	76
6.2 Political rhetoric in speeches, interviews and debates	83

7. Language, power and the law	**98**
7.1 A register rooted in tradition	99
7.2 Functions and features of legal language in written discourse	101
7.3 Spoken language in the courtroom	107
Ideas and answers	**114**
Transcription key	**129**
References	**130**
Glossary	**133**
Index	**135**
Acknowledgements	**136**

Series introduction

Cambridge Topics in English Language is a series of accessible introductory study guides to major scholarly topics in the fields of English language and linguistics. These books have been designed for use by students at advanced level and beyond and provide detailed overviews of each topic together with the latest research in the field so as to provide a clear introduction that is both practical and up to date.

In all of the books in this series, we have drawn on examples of spoken and written language. We hope these will encourage you to apply the theories, concepts and methods that you will learn in the books to analyse data and to think critically about a number of issues and debates relating to language in use. Many of the books also draw on data from the Cambridge Corpus. Throughout each book, you will find short activities to help develop reading and writing skills, longer extended activities and practice questions that will enable you to explore your learning in more detail and research findings that will provide inspiration for your own language investigations. Each of the chapters includes suggested wider reading, and a full glossary and reference section at the end of each book will support you to extend your learning and provide avenues for future reading and research.

We hope that each book will give you a good overview of its topic and, that taken as a whole, the series will map out some of the most interesting and diverse areas of language study, providing you with fresh thinking and new ideas as you embark on your studies.

Dan Clayton

Marcello Giovanelli

How to use this book

Throughout this book you will notice recurring features that are designed to help your learning. Here is a brief overview of what you'll find.

> **Coverage list**
> A short list of what you will learn in each chapter.

> **KEY TERM**
> Definitions of important terms to help your understanding of the topic.

> **ACTIVITY**
> A clearly defined task to help you apply what you've learnt.

> **RESEARCH QUESTION**
> A longer task to help you go deeper into the topic.

> **PRACTICE QUESTION**
> To give you some practice of questions you might encounter in the exam.

Ideas and answers

Further information, suggestions and answers to all activities and practice questions in the book.

Wider reading

Key texts to help extend your learning.

Topic introduction

The association between language and power is around us all every day. Every time we read a billboard, hear a charity appeal on the radio, sit through the advertisement breaks on TV or watch videos on websites, we are being exposed to powerful language. Every time we accept a flyer in the street or pick up a leaflet from the doormat, we will see language and power in action. All these different types of persuasive discourse use similar linguistic techniques to try and influence us. This book explores these linguistic techniques and analyses how language is used so effectively to persuade and influence us.

However, language and power extends beyond being persuasive and influencing our decisions in life. It also positions us within a particular hierarchy. Language can be powerful because it forces us to behave in a certain way. It can be powerful because we use it to reflect on, challenge, reinforce and accept hierarchal roles, status and structures. In this book, you will consider situations where this occurs. Language can exert power within the classroom or within the wide range of workplace environments you may know. It can do so in particular situations such as a consultation with your doctor or an interview with a police officer. This book explores how such contexts affect the language we use and how powerful our language choices are.

The first two chapters cover a wide range of research about language and power, exploring ideas and concepts that will help your understanding of the topic. The remaining chapters then explore these ideas about language in relation to a range of contexts in the media, the workplace, the classroom, politics and the law. The book offers a range of texts* and different activities to help you explore the whole issue of language and power, and give you a full appreciation of how powerful language can be.

*There is a transcription key at the end of the book to help you in your reflections.

Gary Ives

Raj Rana

Chapter 1
Language and power

In this chapter you will:

- Reflect on social inequality and power imbalance in our society

- Understand how language can reflect and challenge inequality and imbalances of power

- Understand how language can affect us positively and negatively

1 Language and Power

This chapter acts as an introduction to the concept that language is powerful, offering an overview of key topics. These topics will subsequently be developed, discussed and evaluated in later chapters.

1.1 Inequality and power imbalance in society

Inequality comes in many very different forms. For example, on the most basic level, there are divisions in wealth, with the rich and the poor living side by side in society. Some argue that the gap is widening with the rich getting richer and the poor getting poorer. The World Bank states that more than a billion people today survive on less than a dollar a day (World Bank, 2012). Oxfam says that in 2015, 50 per cent of the world's wealth was owned by the richest 1 per cent of the population (Elliott, 2017). However, whatever an individual's personal situation regarding money and wealth, people face other inequalities. For example, despite all the advancements in women's rights and the fight for equality with men, there are still differences in our society based on gender. The United Nations Development Programme (UNDP) states that:

> The disadvantages facing women and girls are a major source of inequality. All too often, women and girls are discriminated against in health, education, political representation, labour market, etc — with negative repercussions for development of their capabilities and their freedom of choice. (UNDP, 2015)

Such inequalities in society are, at times, reflected and perpetuated by language. In this chapter we will introduce this link between language and certain power imbalances, focusing on gender, race and class.

1.1.1 Language and gender inequality

Language has, over time, reflected the disadvantages and inequality facing women. Perhaps surprisingly, the use of language by men and women has been studied for centuries. The following quotation is taken from Charles de Rochefort's *Histoire Naturelle et Morale des Iles Antilles de l'Amerique* (*Natural and Moral History of the Antilles Islands of America*) and is based on research carried out in 1665:

> The men have a great many expressions peculiar to them, which the women understand but never pronounce themselves. On the other hand,

the women have words and phrases which the men never use, or they would be laughed to scorn. Thus it happens that in their conversations it often seems as if the women had another language, than the men.

Quoted in Otto Jespersen's *Language: Its Nature, Development and Origin* (1922), Rochefort's research raises some interesting ideas about language and gender which twentieth-century sociolinguists developed. This development has included research into how the English language can be seen as a positioning tool; that is to say how language places women below men within a hierarchal structure. One of the most common examples is the use of 'man' to refer to both sexes in words such as 'mankind'. There is also the generic use of 'he' to refer to both men and women, as well as paired words in which the female version is viewed in a derogatory manner. Take, for example, words which are used to describe promiscuity. In 1977, the linguist Julia Stanley suggested there were 220 terms in English for a promiscuous female and only 20 for a male (Stanley, 1977). Furthermore, the words used for men were often seen as less taboo and often reflected patriarchal societies' views on men and women.

However, things are changing. Gendered words such 'policeman' and 'policewoman' have been replaced by the more neutral 'police officer', whilst words such as 'actress' are being used less and less by the media, instead referring to all as 'actor' regardless of gender. There have also been attempts to combat inequality through pronouns. In Sweden, the introduction of a new single gender-neutral pronoun (*hen*) to replace the Swedish words for 'he' and 'she' has been encouraged in order to minimise gender stereotyping. Published in Sweden in 2012, the children's book *Kivi & Monsterhund* ('Kivi & Monster Dog') was the first to use the new pronoun *hen*. In an article published the same year, Camille Bas-Wohlert discusses how:

> Today, 'han' (he) is automatically used when we don't know the gender of a character and old Swedish rules on writing dictate that 'he' should be used when the sex is not known or is deemed irrelevant – which can be seen in many legal texts. 'Hen' is a solution that makes it possible to meet the world in a more unbiased way and to read a text where the focus is shifted away from gender identity to the personal characteristics of the individual.
> (Bas-Wohlert, 2012)

A further example from England occurred in Brighton in 2012 when the local council suggested the use of the gender-neutral pronoun 'Mx' (short for 'Mixter'). More prevalently in English, there has been an acceptance and growing use of 'they' as a gender-neutral pronoun. Therefore, changes are happening; changes which seek to challenge language and gender inequality.

1 Language and Power

ACTIVITY 1.1
Using gender-neutral pronouns

Discuss and make notes on the attitudes expressed about the use of a gender-neutral title.

> Oh I am delighted about this proposal [in Brighton]. I have been campaigning for years about this. I am not married. I do not want a title. I am me.

> What a lot of rubbish, haven't the [Brighton] council got anything better to do [...]? Real people are Mr Mrs Miss. All this nonsense of Ms as an address is also a lot of rubbish.

> Strictly speaking, there is absolutely no need to call anyone by a title, just a given name will do. But titles are lovely old-fashioned affectations that can define people very positively, for example if you're proud to be married, or you worked years for that PhD. It helps to maintain formality and distance when necessary.

1.1.2 Language and racial inequality

Racial inequality, based on racist attitudes and structural, systemic inequality, is also prevalent across society. A 2016 report by the UK Equality and Human Rights Commission found the following:

- Black people in England are more than three times more likely to be a victim of homicide than those who are white.

- Unemployment rates were 'significantly higher' for ethnic minorities.

- Black workers with degrees earn 23.1% less on average than white employees with the qualifications.

- Ethnic minority people were more likely to live in poverty than white people.

- Ethnic minorities are still 'hugely under-represented' in positions of power – such as judges and police chiefs. (Equality and Human Rights Commission, 2016)

The new field of raciolinguistics analyses the role that language plays in shaping ideas about race. However, 'linguistic racism' (a term that describes when language is used to empower dominant white culture over another racial group) has been an area of study for many years. Robert B. Moore's 'Racism in the English Language' (1976) focuses on how racism is embedded within the English language. He gives examples such as 'Color Symbolism' in which he argues:

> The symbolism of white as positive and black as negative is pervasive in our culture. 'Good guys' wear white hats and ride white horses, 'bad guys' wear black hats and ride black horses. Angels are white, and devils are black. The definition of black includes 'without any moral light or goodness, evil, wicked, indicating disgrace, sinful' while that of white includes 'morally pure, spotless, innocent, free from evil intent'.

Moore also writes about 'Obvious Bigotry', which involves the use of racist slurs which he claims are still commonly used despite 'facing increasing social disdain'.

1.1.3 Language and class inequality

Social class may also act as a discriminating factor within society and the study of class has been a focus for sociolinguists for many years, including a range of research carried out into language use by different social classes. The sociologist Basil Bernstein began his article 'Language and social class' (1960) by claiming that linguistic differences are most marked when the gap between socio-economic levels is great. He argued that there is a difference between the language of the middle class and that of the lower working class. In his article, he discusses how the speech of the latter is limited to a particular form which 'discourages the speaker from verbally elaborating subjective intent and progressively orientates the user to descriptive rather than abstract concepts' (Bernstein 1960: 271–276).

1 Language and Power

Linguistic discrimination is often based on elitist views of language, with people judged on their accent and dialect. This is often linked to class, with those speaking with strong regional (and often working class) accents viewed as inferior to those who speak with an RP accent. As Peter Trudgill (2000) states, 'children with working class accents and dialects may be evaluated by some teachers as having less educational potential than those with middle-class accents and dialects, unless they, too, are given an adequate chance to demonstrate the contrary'.

> **KEY TERMS**
>
> **Accent:** variation in pronunciation associated with a particular geographical region
>
> **Dialect:** variation in words and structures associated with a particular geographical region

1.1.4 Language and other inequalities

There are other groups in society which could also be placed in this pot of inequality; others who feel the pressures of society and may feel like outsiders who are treated differently. Those affected by disability are in one such group. Others may feel unequal due to the prejudices still attached to sexuality. There has been, for example, a recent focus on the use of the word 'gay' to mean 'rubbish'. In an article for *The Guardian* newspaper, the singer Will Young (2013) writes how 'using the word "gay" to mean "crap" is a form of bullying of gay people'. He ends the article by stating, 'Language is key. Language is everything', reinforcing how powerful language can be.

In this unequal world there are certain individuals, groups and institutions that have power over the vast majority and therefore influence society. Simply by following social norms and society's laws, you are accepting this power every day of your life. Language plays a significant role in maintaining this power, acting as a positioning tool to support and reflect hierarchies. Language reinforces stereotypes and can have a significant impact on our everyday lives. It has power over us in so many ways.

1.2 The power of language

Words are powerful. Language is powerful. Its impact on our everyday lives is immeasurable.

Specific choices of words can be offensive to some and evoke negative reactions from others. If language didn't have this power, would a music star be banned from tweeting by their record company? Would a potential US president have

Language and power

his campaign almost de-railed by a recorded conversation using derogatory terms about women? At the heart of these sorts of situations is language – the words chosen by individuals that can have a significant impact on those around them and evoke strong reactions.

Language can be confusing and make people feel isolated too. They may be unfamiliar with the sociolect or dialect of those around them and feel they don't fit in. They may not understand the workplace jargon in a new job and feel like an outsider. They may feel intimidated by the heightened language of individuals whose complex vocabulary appears nonsensical. Language has the power to divide people and to make them feel alienated, frustrated, disaffected and, at times, exasperated.

> **KEY TERM**
>
> **Sociolect:** the language used by a particular social group, e.g. teenage school children, adults in a book club

Of course, language can have a positive effect too. It can encourage, enthuse and motivate. From Martin Luther King's 'I Have a Dream' to Barack Obama's 'Yes we can', political speeches have inspired generations. Stories of personal triumph in the face of adversity make people feel humble and in awe of individuals. The story of Malala Yousafzai, shot by the Taliban as she travelled home from school, was headline news all over the world. Her survival and subsequent public speaking resonated with people of all ages and cultures. Her speech to the United Nations General Assembly led to media outlets across the globe commenting on her words:

'The Assembly listened spellbound to a 16-year-old schoolgirl'

(*The Independent,* 12 July 2013)

'Malala Yousafzai received multiple standing ovations at the United Nations Youth Assembly in New York … and her speech was immediately hailed for its power.'

(*ABC News,* 13 July 2013)

Language can also make people feel personally fulfilled. For example, a charity thanking someone for a kind donation that will save a life acts as a reward for donating a few pounds. Language can make people feel good about themselves – the plethora of gifts adorned with 'World's Greatest Dad/Mum/Granddad/Grandma', for example, help instil that sense of self-worth, love and respect. Kind and thoughtful words written in a greetings card can make the recipient feel emotional and even shed a tear or two. The emotional power of language cannot be underestimated.

1 Language and Power

> **ACTIVITY 1.2**
>
> **The emotional power of language**
>
> Read Text 1A from Amnesty International about the living conditions of refugees. Look at the underlined words and consider which you feel are the most emotional and which are the least. Place the words on a continuum and discuss your ideas with others.

Text 1A

> Over a thousand refugees and migrants, including many children, are living in <u>appalling</u> and <u>unsafe</u> conditions in three camps set up in two old Olympic sites and the arrivals terminal of the unused airport in the Elliniko area, in Athens, Greece's capital. The camps' residents, mostly from Afghanistan, have been living in tents for over a year, enduring <u>very poor</u> hygiene and sanitary conditions, with <u>insufficient</u> toilets and showers, and <u>limited privacy</u>. Residents complain of rats and cockroaches. Humanitarian actors working in the camps are reporting <u>serious</u> mental health problems such as depression, anxiety and suicide attempts, exacerbated by the conditions in the camps.
>
> Amnesty International (2017)

Language is powerful in a wide range of contexts and has so many different outcomes. This has led to many sociolinguists studying the relationship between language and power, and it has become a key area of research.

In the following chapters, you will consider a range of research and findings as you explore various ideas and concepts about the power of language, its key features and its impact in many contexts.

> **RESEARCH QUESTION**
>
> **Language inequality**
>
> Choose one of the areas of language inequality introduced in this chapter. Carry out some research to start to develop a wider understanding of your chosen topic. You could begin by reading about relevant ideas and research; the books and articles in the 'Wider reading' list would make a very good starting point. You can update your research as you learn more about language and power in the subsequent chapters. This could be used as a possible topic for your own investigation or additional study notes for your exam preparation.

Wider reading

You can find out more about the topics in this chapter by reading the following:

Language in society generally

Milroy, L. (1987) *Language and Social Networks* (Second edition). London: Wiley.

Trudgill, P. (2000) *Sociolinguistics: An Introduction to Language and Society*. (revised, Fourth edition). London: Penguin.

Language and power

Brown, P. and Levinson, S. (1987) *Politeness: Some Universals in Language Usage*. Cambridge: Cambridge University Press.

Fairclough, N. (2014) *Language and Power*. (Third edition). London: Longman.

Thomas, L. and Wareing, S. (2012) *Language, Society and Power*. London: Routledge.

Language and social class

Bernstein, B. (1960), British Journal of Sociology, 11 (3): 271–276 'Language and social class'. Available at: www.putlearningfirst.com/language/research/bernstein.html

Milroy, L. and Milroy, J. (1992) *Social Network and Social Class: Toward an Integrated Sociolinguistic Model*. Cambridge: Cambridge University Press.

Attitudes to language

There is a wealth of articles available online which discuss attitudes to language. You may wish to read the following article as an example of what is easily accessible to you. The article is representative of texts which discuss attitudes introduced in this chapter. www.independent.co.uk/arts-entertainment/dilemmas-i-hate-my-sons-workingclass-accent-1106479.html

Clayton, D. (2018) *Attitudes to Language Change and Diversity*. Cambridge: Cambridge University Press.

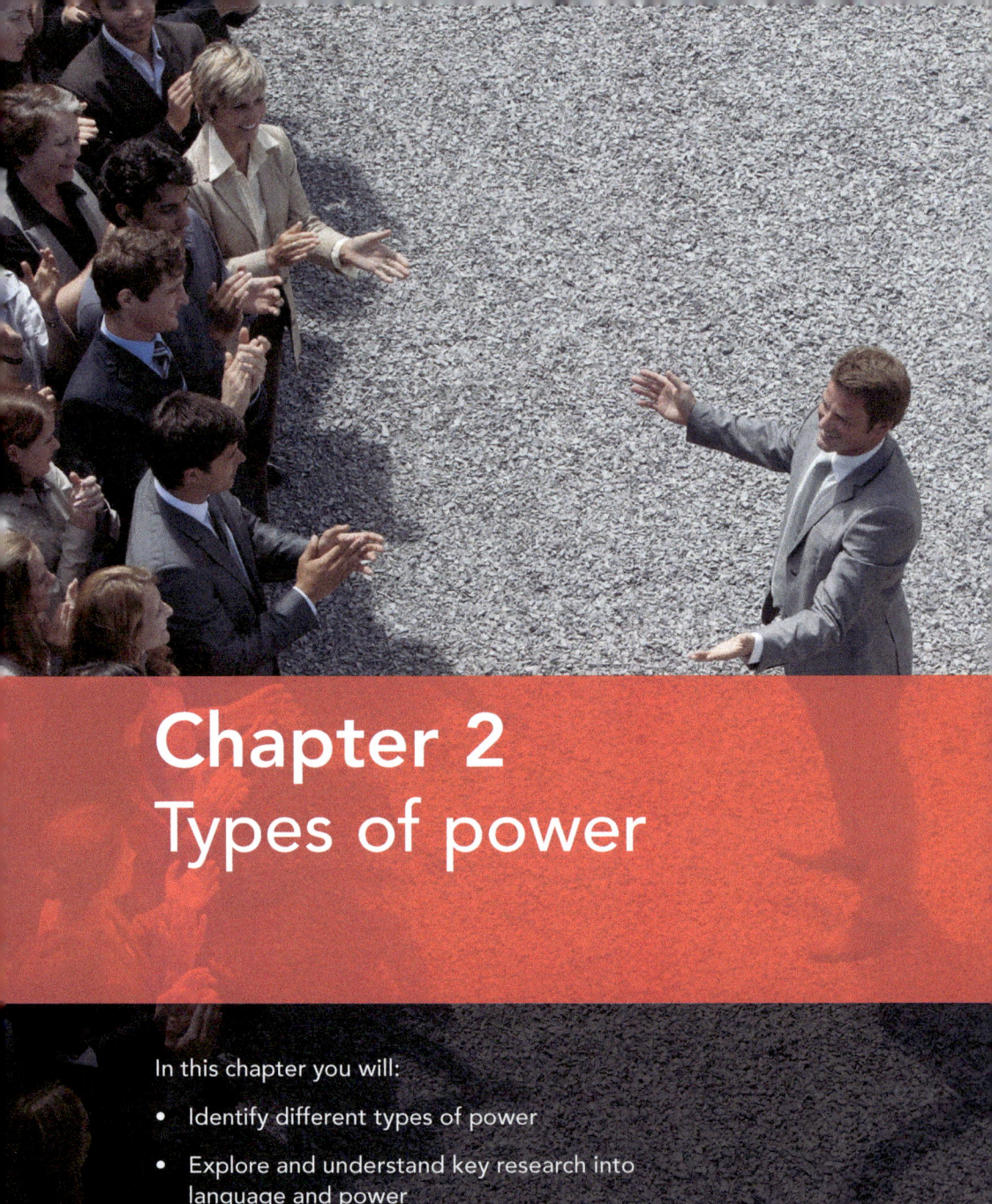

Chapter 2
Types of power

In this chapter you will:

- Identify different types of power

- Explore and understand key research into language and power

This chapter introduces a range of concepts and ideas about power. You will need to have a good understanding of these before exploring how language and power are used in the specific contexts dealt with in Chapters 3–7.

2.1 Concepts about power

2.1.1 Using Critical Discourse Analysis

A key starting point when exploring various ideas and concepts about language and power is Critical Discourse Analysis (CDA), a theory associated with linguists Norman Fairclough and Ruth Wodak. They suggest that even texts which appear to be relatively neutral can actually be loaded with hidden ideological significance. Linguistic strategies are carefully chosen to shape and influence the ways readers might think and feel about particular topics. Fairclough and Wodak (1997) suggest that some of the main areas of concern include:

- social and political issues are constructed and reflected in discourse
- power relations are negotiated and performed through discourse
- discourse both reflects and reproduces social relations
- ideologies are produced and reflected in the use of discourse.

> **KEY TERM**
>
> **Critical Discourse Analysis (CDA):** an approach to the study of written and spoken language focusing on the ways that power is enacted

CDA allows linguists to move beyond a surface understanding of a text so that the relationship between discourse and society can be examined more fully. Exploring this relationship allows the hidden ideologies and values which may underpin dominant discourses to be evaluated and challenged.

Fairclough (1992) devised a three-tiered model for the study of discourse, as shown in Figure 2.1. It illustrates the interconnectedness of discourse analysis: the text is explored within a wider context of production and interpretation.

2 Language and Power

Figure 2.1: The relationship between texts and contexts (adapted from Fairclough 1992)

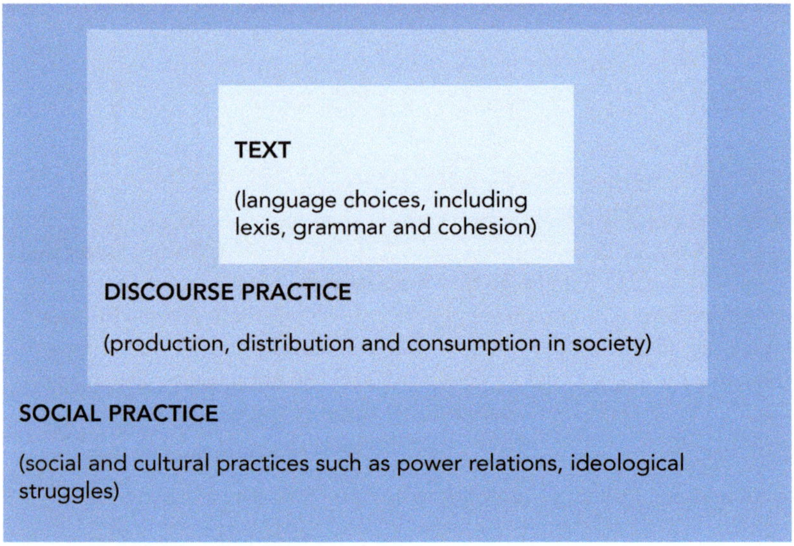

TEXT

(language choices, including lexis, grammar and cohesion)

DISCOURSE PRACTICE

(production, distribution and consumption in society)

SOCIAL PRACTICE

(social and cultural practices such as power relations, ideological struggles)

Applying Fairclough's CDA model can show how language features are used in texts to present particular messages and ideas. Texts can be taken at face value, but examining social and discourse practices helps readers recognise and engage with any underlying messages. These messages may be powerful as they are trying to instruct us or, alternatively, influence us.

In the study of language and power, researchers recognise these different types of power. They identify two main categories: power that *tells* us to do something or power that *persuades* us to do something. This distinction was reinforced by Fairclough (2014) in his use of the terms instrumental power and influential power.

KEY TERMS

Instrumental power: a type of power that is explicit and often imposed by a higher authority

Influential power: a type of power that is persuasive rather than imposing

2.1.2 Instrumental power

Instrumental power is explicit and often imposed by a higher authority. This type of power may be imposed by the government, the legal system, places of work or any type of management. It allows for no choice; there is a clear

Types of power

expectation that people will follow the instructions and that, at times, there will be a consequential penalty if they do not. For example, a poster issued by Cambridge International Examinations states, 'No mobile phones, iPods or MP3/4 players. No products with an electronic communication/storage device or digital facility'. This is not advisory. Students sitting an exam do not have an element of choice here. The rules and regulations are explicit, as is the possible penalty: 'Possession of unauthorised items is an infringement of the regulations and could result in DISQUALIFICATION from this examination and the overall qualification.' The examination board has authority over schools and students in respect of exams. It holds instrumental power and can impose such instructions and penalties.

In this example, the language choices reflect the instrumental power of the examination board. Although there is some slight mitigation via the use of the modal auxiliary verb 'could', lexical choices such as 'unauthorised', 'infringement' and 'disqualification' all echo the power of the board. The receiver will recognise that the consequences are serious because of the language used. The formal register adds to the gravitas of such texts; there is no attempt to converge with the receiver in what tend to be factual statements.

KEY TERMS

Register: a variety of language that is associated with a particular situation of use

Converge: move language styles and patterns to more closely match those of other speakers

ACTIVITY 2.1
Finding examples of instrumental power

Collect your own examples of language that demonstrates instrumental power from your immediate environment. For example, these may include a student contract you signed at the start of your studies or any rules which your school or college shares with students. Then analyse the language in each example and look for patterns of language choices. Do your texts use similar lexical and grammatical features?

2 Language and Power

2.1.3 Influential power

In contrast, influential power tries to make people behave in a certain way, do something particular or change their opinions and attitudes. No 'force' is being applied and there is no penalty for not following any guidance. This type of power is often found in advertising where a persuasive element is vital to success. There may, for example, be an attempt to persuade the receiver to take part in a sales and marketing initiative like this example from Monarch Airlines.

Text 2A

> Win a pair of flights in the Monarch Map Quiz.
>
> Have our fantastic holidays put you in the mood for some sun?
>
> Test your Monarch knowledge and you could be jetting off to one of our stunning sunny destinations.
>
> Look out for the Monarch Map Quiz on Facebook, answer the destination question correctly and you'll be entered into a weekly prize draw!
>
> Yes, we're giving away a pair of flights every week. Don't miss out. Get into the travelling mood with our weekly prize draw!

The register of Text 2A is notably different to that used to show instrumental power. There is clear convergence between the producer and receiver through the use of interrogatives, personal pronouns and informal register. Although the imperatives are not mitigated by politeness markers, they do not appear forceful due to the positive consequences that follow at the end of each sentence; there are no penalties, only rewards. This is common in language used to show influential power. The rewards may be materialistic in the example above but they may also be of a more personal nature. That is to say, the receiver may be made to feel good about themselves or that they will benefit in some way if they go through with what is being suggested. This is certainly the stance taken in recent advertisements to persuade people to enter the teaching profession, after problems with teacher recruitment and retention in the UK.

Text 2B

> Make a difference and inspire the next generation.
>
> You may remember a truly brilliant teacher from school who made a real difference to your life. As a teacher you can use your knowledge and passion for your subject to help children unlock capabilities and talents that they didn't even know they had.
>
> Source: https://getintoteaching.education.gov.uk

Whilst the lexical choices identified in texts that we can identify as demonstrating instrumental power tend to have negative connotations, those in influential texts are in direct contrast and often convey positivity, as in Text 2B. The assumption there is that the reader could be one of these 'truly brilliant teacher[s]' – the noun phrase is used to stir positive memories in the reader and the verb choices 'inspire', 'help' and 'unlock', complemented by the modifier 'real' in 'a real difference', add to the text's influential power. However, there are times when an influential text might use lexis with negative connotations to persuade the receiver. For example, a charity advertising campaign may focus on hard-hitting, emotional facts such as death to meet its purpose. (The power of language in advertising will be further explored in Chapter 3.)

2.1.4 Power behind or power in discourse

Linked to the concept of instrumental and influential power is Fairclough's theory (2014) of whether there is power *behind* discourse or power *in* discourse.

Power behind discourse

When considering the concept of power behind discourse, Fairclough discusses 'social order' and how power 'is enforced by those higher in the institutional hierarchy' and 'imposed upon all … apparently by the … institution or system itself'. In other words, this power behind discourse is created through the known and accepted status inherent in hierarchical structures. It is accepted in many cultures that institutions such as the legal system and the police, and individuals like doctors and heads of organisations, have this type of power. Thus the language they choose to use to others already has power behind it due to their role. The context behind the discourse is what is important. Thus people are extremely likely to trust words from a doctor because society gives doctors a status and gravitas, and accepts their knowledge as being correct. However, even doctors, as well as patients, are themselves subject to the power of the medical institution or system. Doctors are bound by certain rules and regulations imposed by their employer, and patients have to adhere to certain expectations and procedures whilst in a doctor's care.

ACTIVITY 2.2
Finding features of powerful language

Consider Texts 2C and 2D, focusing on the language choices that show power. Text 2C is from the British Medical Association's charter for doctors, linked to published guidance from the General Medical Council (GMC), whilst Text 2D is an extract from the patients' charter of the NABH, an Indian national organisation for hospitals and healthcare providers based in New Delhi.

2 Language and Power

> The use of the modal auxiliary verb 'will' is common in both extracts, reflecting the status and authority of the producer in both cases. The receiver is not given an option. Identify and discuss other specific language features that create power behind the discourse.

Text 2C

Ensuring patient safety and care

Doctors will carry out their duties, workload and work patterns to ensure patient safety and high quality care. Doctors will engage in revalidation, appraisal and job planning processes. They will carry out their duties with care and compassion in compliance with GMC guidance and locally agreed policy and procedures.

From British Medical Association's 'Charter for Doctors'
(www.nhsemployers.org)

Text 2D

Conduct:

- I will respect the doctors and medical staff caring and treating me.
- I will abide by the hospital / facility rules.
- I will bear the agreed expenses of the treatment that is explained to me in advance and pay my bills on time.

Honesty in disclosure:

- I will be honest with my doctor and disclose my family / medical history.

From NABH's 'Patients' Charter'
(nabh.co/images/pdf/Patient_Charter-DMAI_NABH.pdf)

Power in discourse

This type of power relates to *how* powerful participants control others and the tools they use, which links to the idea of inequality discussed in Chapter 1. People encounter a wide range of unequal situations. Using the doctor/patient example once again, the doctor may have power in the discourse through his use of medical terminology or jargon. Fairclough (2014) uses the example of a fully qualified doctor talking to a group of student doctors. Although they all have medical training, the qualified doctor has power over the students. Fairclough notes how often the doctor interrupts the students 'to control the contributions of the student' and how all the orders and questions come from the doctor: 'it appears that the doctor has the right to give orders and ask questions whereas the student only has the obligation to comply and answer'. Thus power in discourse is apparent in unequal encounters and focuses on how the more 'powerful' participant uses various language methods to make their dominance clear to others. The context and accepted roles are also important. In this example, the doctor is likely to have this power in discourse only in a work context and not in a social situation.

Because most people accept the roles of others in society and the authority linked to those roles, everyone is controlled by language in certain situations. Such powerful language might be in the form of instructions from an employer or teachers at school, for example.

KEY TERM

Unequal encounters: when one speaker has accepted dominance over another influencing language choices

The social status of a teacher ensures that the relationship with students is unequal. Although classrooms today are more often seen as places of exchange and collaboration, the relationship remains professional and there are accepted distances which must be maintained by both parties. This manifests itself in stereotypical 'teacher talk' (discussed further in Chapter 5). However, on a general level, a teacher in a classroom situation is more likely to ask questions and give instructions, whilst also giving positive feedback through rewards or praise, as in Text 2E.

Text 2E

Teacher:	just a nice bit of coordinate work to make a start on (.) if you finish the question you are on from the question sheet from your starter wallet (.) right then for question was it question one you should've got was it a triangle
Students:	yeah
Teacher:	yeah (.) what type was it (1) Jude
Jude:	was it an isosceles
Teacher:	isosceles excellent (1) right one for question well it was question two actually wasn't it (.) Joseph please don't darling (1) what is the name of the shape on question 2 stroke 3 then (.) Grace
Grace:	um was it a um rhombus

2 Language and Power

Teacher:	um I think it is actually (2) actually a kite is it not (2) a rhombus (1) what's special about a rhombus (.) all the three sides are (.) go on
Grace:	is it that all the sides are the same (1) length
Teacher:	yeah all the sides are the same length aren't they and that that shape that quadrilateral I think is a kite because they aren't all the same size (1) ok so if you put the sheets back inside your starter wallet (2) can you get your orange books out and turn to last week's work (.) well we blew our minds talking about straight graphs (.) it was (4) I think we all left thankful it was the weekend but fortunately we are going to crack at it and crack it today (1) this little diagram is what we're starting on (1) can you all find that yeah (1) joseph what have I asked you to do (5) ok so can you all find that little diagram the y = 6x (2) let's have a look Tommy (1) excellent (2) where's that diagram we did on Friday (1) oh did you go early
Tommy:	yeah
Teacher:	excuses excuses excuses (1) we'll sort it out in a bit (1) right (2) on Friday's lesson then we discovered (1) can you just look at this board we looked at graphs in the form y = nx + c a number in front of the x and a number at the end (1) anybody remember (1) for example y = 2x + 6 can anyone remember what that 2 stands for what is its significance of that number there (1) Kelsey
Kelsey:	gradient
Teacher:	oh wow (1) absolutely brilliant vocab (.) gradient (1) what does that word gradient mean (1) Leon
Leon:	is it the is it how far it goes up
Teacher:	excellent so it's the steepness

This transcript shows many of the language features Fairclough identified as evidence of power in discourse. For example, the teacher holds the conversational floor by:

- steering and dominating the conversation with the students

- directing and controlling the conversation, inviting specific students to speak and respond but only when asked

- asking the questions throughout whilst at times not giving the students opportunities to respond.

There is also evidence of the teacher:

- using some turn-yielding cues such as the pauses when she asks a question ('so can you all find that little diagram the y = 6x (2) let's have a look Tommy').
- praising the students as a way of exerting her power over them – she has the authority to give out praise, and recognise and reward correct responses.

All these language features are used by the teacher because of her role in this unequal encounter. You could argue that students expect their teachers to use powerful language features and accept them due to the established hierarchy. If a teacher did not use these features, how would a student respond? Would the respect disappear?

KEY TERMS

Holding the conversational floor: speaking until the speaker finished what they wish to say or until someone interrupts them

Turn-yielding cue: when a speaker invites and encourages others in a conversation to respond, thus relinquishing control; this can be through pausing, intonation or lexical cues such as 'I think' and 'you know'

ACTIVITY 2.3
Exploring language choices for a positive climate

Discuss how the teacher in Text 2E uses different forms of power in the classroom to create a positive climate for learning in her classroom.

Think about your own experiences in the classroom. Do your teachers use similar techniques? Which do you find the most effective?

2.1.5 Political, personal and social group power

Various researchers have identified other types of power that complement Fairclough's concepts. Shan Wareing (Thomas and Wareing, 1999) divided power into three main types:

- political
- personal
- social group.

2 Language and Power

She summarises these distinct types of power:

> One way we see power at work in society is through politics. By means of our vote in a democracy we give politicians the right to make laws on our behalf. If we break those laws, society has the power to punish us. 'Political power' controls many aspect of our lives: how much we pay in taxes, what our healthcare and education is like, how fast we can drive and many other areas and activities. This power is reinforced through individuals such as police officers, judges and prison officers, whose jobs give them the right to affect other people's lives. Other people who have power as a consequence of their roles include teachers, parents and employers. We can classify this type of power as 'personal power'. Finally some social groups have more of less power than others. The poor, the disabled, ethnic minorities and women are all groups which may find themselves having lower social status, fewer economic resources, and being discriminated against. Typically, the people with most 'social group power' are white, wealthy and male.
> (Thomas and Wareing 1999: 11)

The question then is how this power links to language.

Political power and language

Political language certainly has a distinct register (discussed in Chapter 6), politicians exert power through their speeches and parliamentary debates, and institutions and individuals (such as police officers) give direct orders through their language. There is a link here to Fairclough's theories of instrumental power and power behind discourse. Society accepts the existence of this type of power and that the language used is appropriate given the status of the individuals or institutions involved.

Personal power and language

The acceptance of personal power is also ingrained in society as it links to the idea of unequal encounters in which one party has dominance over another. The way a parent or care-giver speaks to a child is an example of this, although the level of acceptance perhaps becomes blurred during teenage years! However, it is certainly evident in early years when the adult and child have very distinct roles. Important research (Ringler, 1981; Cameron-Faulkner, Lieven and Tomasello, 2003; Field, 2004) into child-directed speech (CDS) has studied the way adults speak to children and shows that parents and care-givers use specific linguistic features in this unequal encounter. The key features include:

- using the child's name as well as personal nouns when talking about oneself (e.g. 'Mummy will go and get Abigail a drink' rather than 'I'll go and get you a drink')

- speaking in a higher pitch than normal, with a 'singsong' intonation to emphasise key words.

However, is this type of language powerful? Research does not tend to focus on this – articles about CDS are usually focused on child language development rather than power. However, given Wareing's definition of personal power, it is relevant. When an adult takes on the role to help develop a child's language, they choose language to pursue that aim. They know that young children respond to pitch, tone and inflection, and they will also use other features of CDS that support language development. Using these features gives the adult the power to help the child acquire language. What could be more powerful than helping someone develop the power of speech?

Of course the personal power of a care-giver is not just evident in a child's early years. It develops as the child gets older. The language used by the care-giver changes so that the powerful role is maintained. Guidance is even available to care-givers on how to use language to speak to their children. Sandra Schumer (2014) states, 'None of us rise in the morning with the attitude: "Today I will try to make my child feel guilty, stupid, incapable, worthless, unimportant, weak or unloved." However, despite our best efforts, sometimes even before breakfast … we have succeeded in accomplishing at least one or perhaps all of the above.' What follows is advice on how the reader can avoid these situations and improve their role as a care-giver and, in line with Wareing's theory, their personal power. As Schumer declares in her introduction, 'I offer an understanding of communication and the power of words'.

Social group power and language

When considering social group power, Wareing (Thomas and Wareing, 1999) makes reference to some of the groups mentioned in Chapter 1 of this book. She recognises that certain groups in society have lower status and that other groups have power. The divide, in her view, is linked to wealth, ethnicity and gender.

Researchers from the University of California (Kraus and Keltner 2009) have studied how those born into wealth and privilege communicate. They studied videotapes of 50 conversations between pairs of strangers. They found that wealthier people were far more likely to appear distracted when talking; they were, for example, more likely to fidget and doodle. In contrast, those at the other end of the wealth scale were far more attentive and made far more of an effort to engage in conversation. The research concluded that this may be because the wealthy don't feel the need to make a good impression whilst those who are less well-off are anxious to come across well. Thinking about Wareing's theory, one could draw the conclusion that these wealthier people don't feel the need to make an effort because they know they have social group power whilst the poorer participants are aware that they do not and therefore feel the need to try more. The wealthier people are not being rude but are behaving this way in conversation because they are rich and they know the benefits associated with this. It's a possible interpretation.

2 Language and Power

Gregory R. Guy (1988: 37) argues that differences in social prestige, wealth and power are some of the most important sociolinguistic divisions which impact on language. He argues that people show their social differences through their phonology, grammar and lexical choices. As a basic example, he refers to how professors don't sound like plumbers, claiming that they 'signal the social differences between them by features of the phonology, grammar and lexical choice'.

The research done at the University of California and by Guy is linked to Wareing's concept of social group power by the idea that in an unequal society different groups use different forms of language. It could also be argued that the language used by those with social group power is seen as more prestigious. Attitude to language is an important factor to consider when looking at power. Are those seen as having less power being discriminated against because of their language? (See *Attitudes to Language*, *Language Change*, *Diversity in English and World Englishes* and *Language Diversity* in this series.) Consider Text 2F, the opening of an online article published in The Lawyer. You can read the full article at www.cambridge.org/links/escpow6006

Text 2F

> The UK's top law firms are rejecting well-qualified candidates because their accents are too 'working class', according to a new study.
>
> Research carried out by the Cass Business School shows that while elite firms have made strides on increasing recruitment of ethnic minorities into their ranks, working class applicants miss out because they do not fit with the brand.
>
> A partner at one of five case study firms, all of which are in the UK top 20, told Cass Business School: "There was one guy who came to interviews who was a real Essex barrow boy, and he had a very good CV, he was a clever chap, but we just felt that there's no way we could employ him. I just thought, putting him in front of a client – you just couldn't do it."
>
> From Margaret Taylor, 'Top firms reject candidates with 'working class' accents', *The Lawyer*, 21 December 2010

The article continues by suggesting that those from social groups which Wareing would argue have power dominate the legal profession. Once again, the focus is on inequality and how language can, in some ways, reinforce such inequality and prevent things from changing.

2.1.6 Powerful language

Teun van Dijk, a professor of discourse studies, has also written about power and control in language. According to van Dijk, people often create an asymmetrical relationship with others through their use of language. So called 'powerful' language can be used to influence or instruct others. Van Dijk argues that everyone has 'personal' power, stemming from certain speech patterns, in how they speak and know when (and when not) to speak. He cites the example that two people might say the same thing, yet one is far more believable because of how they say it. As van Dijk (2008) states, 'If what one says is always worth listening to, then whenever one speaks, those that know you will listen'. He also gives the example of someone wanting to contribute to a conversation but being unsure of when to speak and thus staying silent. This, according to van Dijk, makes people feel powerless.

Van Dijk also discusses how power stems from roles in society, which links to both Fairclough and Wareing's ideas. He gives the example of a dialogue between a doctor and a patient in which, through socialisation, the patient adheres to certain expectations. The patient may, for example, let the doctor hold the conversational floor, initiate topics and lead a question/answer discourse structure. However, if the patient met the doctor in a different social context, they would act differently and not allow the doctor to have this same power.

ACTIVITY 2.4
Roles and social contexts

Consider the following scenarios between a father and his 18-year-old son. Discuss how language may change in the different contexts depending on the role of each speaker.

- At school where the son is one of the father's students
- On the football pitch where the son is captain of the amateur team that he and his father play for

2.1.7 Positive power

It is clear that much of the research into types of power focuses on asymmetrical relationships. This could seem to highlight the problems of an unequal society as a negative thing. However, in his book *Power: A Radical View* (1974), Steven Lukes argues that this is not always the case. He focused on the whole concept of power as domination and discussed how the powerful secure the compliance (willing or unwilling) of those they dominate. He calls this concept 'power over' but argues that not all types of 'power over' are negative or have an adverse effect on the subordinate party: 'power over others can be productive, transformative, authoritative and compatible with dignity'. He gives the example of a typical asymmetrical relationship – teacher and student – and argues that this is not always a relationship of domination but can be transformative for both parties. The student learns and improves intellectually and academically. In turn, the teacher can also develop and learn from the student. This is certainly an interesting take on the whole concept of power between two unequal sections of society and challenges some of the ideas put forward by Wareing and van Dijk.

2.2 Politeness as a power tool

Politeness in speech can also be linked to types of power. One of the most notable pieces of research in this area is sociologist Erving Goffman's face theory, later developed by Penelope Brown and Stephen Levinson in their research on positive and negative politeness.

The concept of face-work was first discussed in Goffman's paper 'On face-work: an analysis of ritual elements of social interaction' (1967). Whilst the idea was not new (Goffman drew on Chinese and American Indian publications dating back to 1894, which focused on 'face' being linked to the regard one person has for another based on their moral reputation), he further developed the concept with a focus on interaction and communication. To Goffman, everyone wants to show a particular public image and this manifests itself in how they communicate with others. Any individual will have different 'faces', depending on a particular context, but whatever 'face' they are showing they want it to be in line with social values and society's expectations. Thus a teacher will have a particular 'face' whilst in the classroom and will communicate in an appropriate way. However, once out of this role, the 'face' will change.

This relates to types of power through the concept of face-threatening acts (FTAs), developed by Penelope Brown and Stephen Levinson (1987) from Goffman's idea of face. They argued that face can be threatened by three issues: power, distance and rank.

> ### KEY TERMS
> **Face-work:** Goffman's term for the behaviours used in presenting or protecting our face to others, as well as those that show our respect of other speakers' 'faces'
>
> **Face-threatening act:** a speech act that has the potential to damage someone's self-esteem

- **Power:** In this case, power refers to the perceived power dynamic between two people (whether one is superior, more subordinate or on the same level) and an individual's face can be threatened if they are spoken to in a way that is not appropriate given the power dynamic. For example, if a student makes fun of a teacher, they are carrying out an FTA. In another context, for example, if the teacher was at home and their own children were making fun of them, this might not be an FTA. This links to the research discussed on asymmetrical relationships and the accepted expectations of status and hierarchy.

- **Distance:** Goffman's idea of distance refers to the social distance between two people; for example, whether speaking to a colleague or a close friend. He argues that if language choices do not reflect this distance, the speaker is carrying out an FTA. For example, being overly familiar and sharing personal information with a colleague will threaten their face. They may be offended by what is said or may simply feel it is inappropriate.

- **Rank:** This might suggest a further link to hierarchy and status, but Goffman used it to refer to how a topic is perceived in different cultures and which topics might be more sensitive to discuss than others.

Brown and Levinson identified two different kinds of face that could be threatened: positive face and negative face.

- **Positive face:** 'the want of every member that their wants be desirable to at least some others' (Brown and Levinson, 1987: 62). In other words, everyone wants to be liked by others. Positive FTAs might include speaking rudely to someone, disagreeing or arguing with them, or constantly interrupting during a conversation.

- **Negative face:** 'the want of every competent adult member of a community that their actions be unimpeded by others' (Brown and Levinson, 1987: 62). That is to say, no one wants to be imposed on. A good example of a negative FTA is when one person is over-friendly with someone they don't have a close relationship with.

Brown and Levinson developed these ideas further with the concept of positive and negative politeness and associated strategies.

- **Positive politeness:** This is used in an attempt to ensure someone's positive face is maintained to make the listener feel good about themselves and establish friendliness and camaraderie. Strategies include giving compliments, listening intently and giving cues to communicate interest to the speaker. They may also include using in-group language to establish a shared identity or using terms of address that suggest closeness (for example, 'mate', 'pal', 'dude', 'bro', etc.).

- **Negative politeness:** This is used in an attempt to avoid the negative FTA of imposing on someone. Strategies include apologising for bothering someone by beginning a conversation with 'Sorry to bother you, but have you got a minute?', for example.

2 Language and Power

It would seem that, regardless of any asymmetry in the power dynamic of a relationship, people accept the desire and need to use negative and positive politeness. It could be argued that politeness is key regardless of who has the power and also that being polite gives a speaker some power in a conversation. On the other hand, engaging in FTAs exercises power through dominance and could be a way of challenging expected behaviour in communication.

> **ACTIVITY 2.5**
> Using politeness
>
> Consider the following scenarios and discuss how the end result could be achieved through politeness:
>
> - You want to borrow some money from your parents.
>
> - You want your parents to pick you up at midnight after going to a late cinema screening.
>
> - You want your parents to let you go away for the weekend without them.

2.3 Power and genre

A final aspect of power that it is important to understand, before considering the various contexts which follow in this book, is genre. That is to say, what are the key features of power which are common in certain genres? For the purpose of exploring the contexts in Chapters 3–7, it is useful to focus on the broader genres of speech and writing. Tables 2.1–2.3 give an overview of the power features that are most common in speech and writing. You will see that there is, of course, some overlap. All these features will be developed in the rest of the book, as you learn which of them are more common in particular contexts and about the impact they have. As you explore further, you will begin to see patterns emerge.

> **KEY TERM**
>
> **Genre:** a way of grouping texts based on expected shared conventions

Types of power

Table 2.1: Power in speech

Feature	The person with power…
Initiating/Topic initiation	… is more likely to start the conversation and introduce new topics.
Topic shifts	… is more likely to change the subject in a conversation, moving from one topic to another.
Topic management	… is more likely to control (or manage) the subject of the whole conversation.
Holding the floor	… is more likely to dominate the conversation by talking more.
Overlaps and interruptions	… may dominate by trying to take over the conversation.

Table 2.2: Power in writing

Feature	The producer with power…
Logo	… may include a logo in the text; this will indicate power or authority, may be recognised by the receiver and can add a sense of gravitas.
Graphology	… may include images to reinforce their purpose. For example, an image of a malnourished child might persuade the receiver to support a charity.
Discourse	… may structure their text in a way that reflects their power, authority or purpose. For example, very dense text with few breaks may be daunting to the receiver and put them off reading the detail. Conversely, text that is broken up into short paragraphs, with images and text boxes, will invite the receiver to read it more carefully and perhaps be persuaded to follow its recommendations.

Language and Power

Table 2.3: Power in speech and writing

Feature	If the person with power…
Conditional	… uses a conditional construction, the receiver is often given consequences that could be positive ('If you donate today, you will save a life') or more negative ('If you exceed the limit, you will be fined').
Imperative	… gives orders, a sense of power and authority can be established ('Look this way').
Mitigated imperative	… softens an order, the receiver may be more likely to respond in the manner intended by the producer ('Please sign and return your contract').
Modifiers	… adds extra description, the receiver may be more likely to respond in the manner intended by the producer ('The poor, starving child…').
Modal verbs	… uses modal verbs of compulsion, the receiver may feel there are no options ('You must return this item within 14 days').
Direct address	… uses direct address, the receiver may be more likely to respond accordingly ('You can make a difference').
Inclusive pronouns	… uses first-person pronouns to create a sense of unity, the receiver may be more likely to respond accordingly ('Join us in our campaign').

RESEARCH QUESTION
Types of power

Go back to the research task you started in Chapter 1 but now think about the concepts covered in this chapter. Can you make links to any of the types of power covered in Chapter 2 to add further detail to your work? You will find it useful to refer to the books in the wider reading list.

Wider reading

You can find out more about the topics in this chapter by reading:

Critical Discourse Analysis

Fairclough, N. (2013) *Critical Discourse Analysis: The Critical Study of Language*. London: Routledge.

Paltridge, B. (2008) *Discourse Analysis.* London: Continuum Discourse Series.

Language and power

Brown, P. and Levinson, S. (1987). *Politeness: Some Universals in Language Usage*. Cambridge: Cambridge University Press.

Fairclough, N. (2014) *Language and Power*. (Third edition). London: Longman.

Newmeyer, F. J. (ed.) (1989) *Language: The Socio-Cultural Context (Linguistics: The Cambridge Survey, Volume 4)*. Cambridge: Cambridge University Press.

Thomas, L. and Wareing, S. (2012) *Language, Society and Power*. London: Routledge.

Chapter 3
Language, power and the media

In this chapter you will:

- Develop an understanding of the language used by journalists

- Evaluate the power of language in advertising

- Explore how emotive language is used by charities

3.1 Access to the media

The term 'media' encompasses the main means of mass communication. It once referred only to publishing, which produced printed formats such as newspapers, books and articles. Then advances in technology brought the ability to broadcast news, documentary and drama on radio and television. Now technology gives us instant access to every type of digital format on the internet, including news, opinions, games and films, which are available on a wide range of devices such as laptops, tablets and mobile phones. All these different manifestations of media are now part of our day-to-day lives.

The rapid rise in the use of smartphones and tablets has expanded our constant exposure to the media. Next time you're on a bus or train, just count how many commuters are sitting reading or watching something on their phone. Without doubt, it will be a significant number. Alternatively, survey your peers on how much they access the media and the methods they use. Our habits are changing as we switch more and more to accessing the media whilst 'on the go', as shown in the data in Figure 3.1 from the UK Office for National Statistics.

Figure 3.1: Devices used to access the internet in the UK in 2016

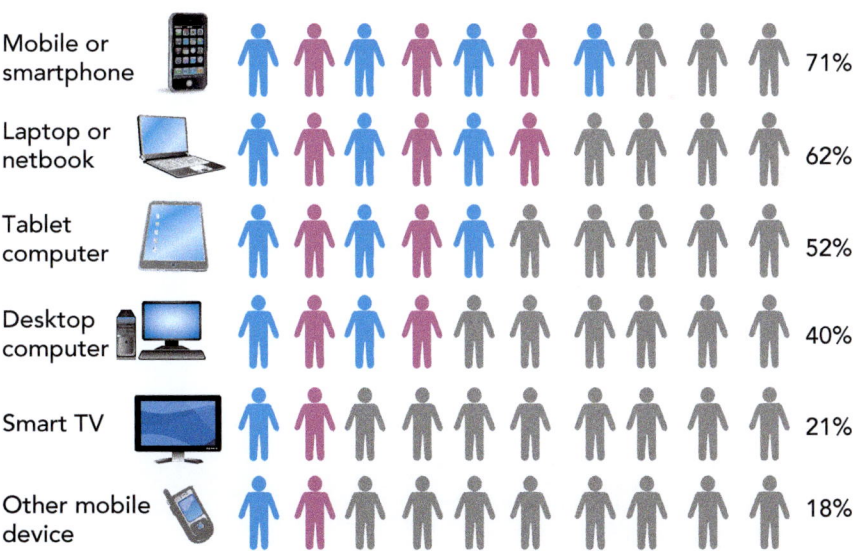

Source: Office for National Statistics, 2016

The percentage of adults who access the internet 'on the go' has doubled since 2011 (Office for National Statistics, 2016). This corresponds with a decline in the circulation of newspapers as people switch to other media platforms

Language and Power

to access the news. Therefore, times are changing. However, what remains constant is the importance and influence of the media on our lives. This chapter explores three key areas, considering how the language they use can be powerful:

- journalism
- advertising
- charity appeals.

3.2 The language and power of journalism

The role of journalists can vary. You might assume their job is to report the news in a factual, impartial manner. However, this is not always the case. Whilst journalists may communicate facts to readers and listeners, they may also be trying to influence views and opinions. Whilst this would be expected in editorials, for example, it might be less easy to believe that it is inherent in news reporting too.

Stuart Hall (1973) introduced the concept of audience positioning. He suggests that all media texts are 'encoded' by the producer to contain certain meanings, which are then 'decoded' by the receiver/audience. He suggests there will be three readings:

- Dominant readings: the audience accepts the text and will interpret the text in the same way in which the producer of the text intended.
- Negotiated readings: the audience understands what the text is trying to achieve but they don't relate to it.
- Oppositional or resistant readings: the audience rejects the text itself due to their beliefs or experiences.

> **KEY TERM**
>
> **Audience positioning:** the assumptions made in a text about its readers' background knowledge and understanding, attitudes and values in order to guide them towards an interpretation

This section will consider how the language choices journalists make contribute to the power they have to influence, manipulate and position their audience.

3.2.1 'Mass communication or mass manipulation?'

In 2016 Shalini Singh, an award-winning journalist from India, tried to deliver a speech in Delhi entitled 'Mass communication or mass manipulation?', echoing current research and debate on communication versus manipulation in journalism. Although she was interrupted and stopped from giving the full speech, Singh has subsequently published it. She debates the role of journalists in reporting news events and begins by arguing that:

> While it's fair to say that both communication and manipulation coexist in the media, the taint of manipulation has been growing stronger… while the role of any journalist should be to relentlessly work for meaningful change, eventually leading to the upliftment of humanity. A journalist's only obligation is to the truth. Truth that can be verified in public interest. And journalism is only reliable when it is delivered by a journalist who is independent in mind and spirit. (Singh 2016)

According to Singh, journalists should present an impartial, accurate and truthful version of events. However, she accepts that this is not always the route journalists take. She concludes:

> The real question to be asked in the cacophony of these times is how many people are willing to step forward to truly and joyfully choose the path of service – in this case, mass communication – rather than the path of professional advancement or the path of mass manipulation? (Singh 2016)

This question seems to suggest that those who choose the former path are in the minority.

In 1991, at the start of the first Gulf War, *The Guardian* newspaper carried out research that tried to evidence the whole concept of communication versus manipulation. Over the period of the first week of the war, the newspaper tracked the use of language from national newspapers. In an article titled 'Mad Dogs and Englishmen', the newspaper published its findings. The key points are shown in Table 3.1.

Table 3.1: Communication versus manipulation in war reporting

We have…	Army, Navy and Air Force	They have…	A war machine
We…	Take out	They…	Destroy
	Suppress		Destroy
	Eliminate		Kill
	Neutralise		Kill

3 Language and Power

We launch…	First strikes	They launch…	Sneak missile attacks
	Pre-emptively		Without provocation
Our men are…	Boys	Their men are…	Troops
	Lads		Hordes
Our boys are…	Professional	Their boys are…	Brainwashed
	Cautious		Cowardly
	Dare-devils		Cannon fodder
	Young knights of the sky		Bastards of Baghdad
	Loyal		Blindly obedient
	Brave		Fanatical
Our missiles cause…	Collateral damage	Their missiles cause…	Civilian casualties

Source: From 'Mad Dogs and Englishmen', *The Guardian*, 23 January 1991

It is clear when looking at the semantics of the language used, that the English army and soldiers are presented in a far more positive light than their Iraqi counterparts. For example, the use of the modifier 'loyal' to describe British soldiers conjures up images of dependable, patriotic service personnel who are dedicated to protecting their country. They are carrying out the duties they signed up for. In contrast, the phrase 'blindly obedient' has connotations of the opponent's soldiers being almost unaware of what they are doing as if brainwashed into compliance. There does not seem to be the same sense of duty as created by the modifier 'loyal'. Thus *The Guardian* found that the British press was not simply communicating the facts of the war; it was, in fact, manipulating its audience.

ACTIVITY 3.1
Semantics of war
Choose some other examples from Table 3.1 and explain what you believe the journalists were trying to achieve. How do they present the British and Iraqi forces?

Language, power and the media

Front covers and headlines

Of course it is not uncommon for newspapers to take a particular political stance. In the run-up to general elections in the UK, most of the daily newspapers decide to support one party over another. In the general election in 2015, two of the biggest selling tabloid newspapers supported different parties and their front page coverage on the day after the election when the Conservative Party (Tories/'The Blues') had won (Texts 3A and 3B) was certainly indicative of their stance.

Text 3A

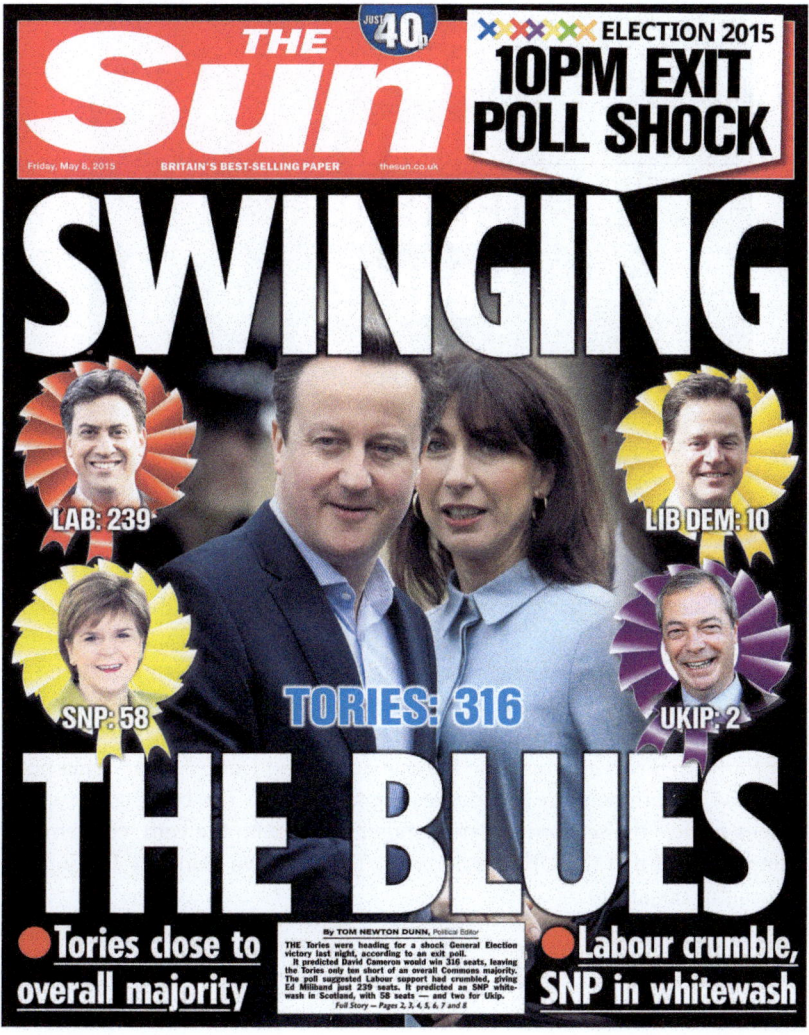

3 Language and Power

Text 3B

The Sun chose to use a pun on the song 'Singing the Blues' as their headline, evoking a positive and uplifting tone. It also used positive images, choosing pictures of smiling politicians (including those who had been defeated) to perhaps further emphasise the newspaper's joyful response to the result. This mood is juxtaposed with the verb 'crumble', chosen to describe the performance of the Labour Party. In direct contrast, the Labour-supporting *Daily Mirror* could not have printed a more negative and depressing front page. The black cover with no images reflects the sombre and despondent mood with the verb 'condemned' reflecting its belief that the UK was doomed. The adjective 'damned' further reinforces this negativity.

Such opposing political stances are not, of course, limited to the UK. In the US, newspapers also tend to side with one party over another. In 2012, US newspapers were split roughly half and half in their endorsement for

Language, power and the media

Barack Obama or Mitt Romney. However, in the run up to the 2016 American Presidential election, the split in newspaper support for the candidates was very different. In October 2016, it was reported that only six newspapers across the whole of the country had publicly endorsed Donald Trump (Arrieta-Kenna, 2016). In contrast, over 200 newspapers endorsed Hillary Clinton. As history now tells us, the result of the election did not match this unprecedented difference in endorsements, which raises a question: Just how powerful and influential are newspapers? They may try to manipulate our feelings and emotions, but can they really influence such major choices in life?

Trump's victory in the election is likely to be one of the most divisive events of our generation, with many media outlets across the world critical of the election result to quite an exceptional degree. The headlines and other statements from international newspapers in Table 3.2 show evidence of journalists trying to manipulate their readers by sharing their own views and opinions, rather than simply reporting the facts. The example headlines range from the humorous take on the acronym 'WTF' to the far more serious take on Obama's rallying cry 'Yes we can' with the 'No You Can't' headline from New Zealand.

Table 3.2: Front page headlines from around the world on the results of the 2016 US presidential election

Newspaper	Headline	Other statements
Daily News, New York	House of Horrors	Wide revulsion signals national nightmare
VG, Norway	Bloody Serious for Norway	
Libération, France	Trumpocalypse	
Daily Telegraph, Australia	W.T.F.	Will Trump Flourish
Daily Telegraph, Australia	God Save America	The US presidential nightmare
L'Echo, Belgium	American Psycho	
New Zealand Herald	Dear America… No You Can't!	
I, United Kingdom	Disunited States	

Naming and referencing

In addition to front pages and headlines, journalists can also try to influence their readers through naming – that is to say, how they decide to refer to individuals. In two separate articles published side by side, journalists wrote about a rather infamous boy. In the first article, the headline referred to the boy as 'My

3 Language and Power

Little Friend', where the modifier 'little' might elicit feelings of innocence and vulnerability. In the opening sentence, he is referred to solely by his first name Robert. Subsequently he is referred to as Bobby (which possibly makes him more personable to the reader) and as one of the 'residents' in the place where he lives. In contrast, the second article, 'The Child Killer' makes it far clearer who the journalists are writing about. Robert/Bobby is not 'my little friend' but 'the Child Killer'. This noun phrase in the headline could be read two ways – he has killed a child or he is a child who has killed. In fact both fit the person being written about. In the second headline, the use of the noun 'child', normally associated with the innocence and vulnerability alluded to in the first headline, takes on a far more sinister meaning. This child is no longer just Robert or Bobby but is referred to by his full name Robert Thompson or, later in the article, by just his surname.

Both articles are about one of the most disturbing crimes of recent times in the UK – the murder of two-year-old James Bulger in February 1993 by Thompson and his friend, who were only ten years old at the time. Instead of trying to create sympathy for Thompson, as the first article does, the choice of words in the second article positions the audience to relate more to the plight of James Bulger. In the second article, the murdered boy is referred to as 'James', 'little James' and 'two year old James'. The references to his age and size have clearly been chosen by the journalist to provoke different emotions in the reader – sympathy for James' family and revulsion for those who killed him.

As well as naming, both journalists use a range of emotive language. In the first article, the journalist tries to make readers feel sorry for Thompson by using the modifiers 'shy' and 'ordinary' and the noun phrases 'a nice lad' and 'celebrity offender'. In contrast, the second article refers to him as someone whose name 'became synonymous with wickedness'; he is described as 'a killer' and the verb 'battered' is used to describe the killing. These two articles show so clearly how journalists can use language to present such different opinions, even of the same person. What is left out by the first journalist is also interesting; there is no reference to the crime but all focus is on how Thompson is coping whilst being detained.

In his book *Analysing Newspapers* (2006), John Richardson also discusses this journalistic method of naming and reference. He quotes a study by Clark (1992) which examined the way *The Sun* newspaper reported incidents of sexual violence and how the articles often held up one of the participants as being to blame whilst the other was the victim. Clark found that gender played a significant role in the language chosen. If the man was seen as the one to blame, he was a 'monster', a 'maniac', a 'fiend' or a 'beast'. However, if the article laid the blame on the woman she was referred to as an 'unmarried mum', 'a divorcee' or by using adjectives relating to her physical appearance: 'busty', 'shapely', 'blonde'. As Richardson states '"Busty divorcees" are never attacked by fiends; instead, the men who attack "busty divorcees" are represented as blameless and are described by name or using respectable terms, like "family man" or proximate colloquial terms like "hubby"' (Richardson, 2006). Richardson argues that *The Sun* creates a situation through language whereby 'bad men attack innocent women [whilst] bad women provoke innocent men'.

The Sun has also been subject to one of the most famous cases of a newspaper trying to influence their readers – their coverage of the Hillsborough disaster. In 1989, 96 football supporters were killed in a tragic incident when they were crushed in a standing-only area of the stadium. The front page *The Sun* decided to run after the disaster has become synonymous with how journalists can distort the facts, ironic given that the headline *The Sun* chose was 'The Truth'. In the article, the concept of naming/referencing was used to vilify the football fans caught up in the accident. They were described as: 'drunken fans', 'hooligan element', 'thugs' and 'animals'. It is known now, of course, that none of this was true and the editor at the time subsequently called the inaccuracy a fundamental mistake. The subsequent reaction to the story was immense. Newsagents in Liverpool refused to stock the newspaper and still today many boycott the tabloid in protest of its story. The power of journalism is evident for all – in their reporting, *The Sun* isolated and angered many.

Figure 3.2: Many people protested about the way *The Sun* reported the Hillsborough disaster

Such manipulation is not, of course, restricted to newspapers. The media is an ever-expanding entity and newspapers are perhaps no longer the most influential player. Social media platforms such as Facebook, Twitter and even YouTube have become alternative sources of news for many people, while blogs have also served as ways for journalists and writers to reach an audience directly without being mediated by established news organisations. However, the veracity and accuracy of the information, or the credentials - or even actual physical existence - of the writers is harder to determine.

3.2.2 Impartial reporting

There are, of course, media outlets that do try to remain impartial and to communicate facts in the way advocated by Singh. In the UK, the BBC's editorial guidelines highlight the importance of impartiality and how the channel needs to be inclusive, reflecting its wide audience and their differing views and opinions.

However, can any journalist or media outlet ever remain totally impartial? Even with the best intentions, surely some form of personal opinion or viewpoint will surface? Given the number of complaints made about the BBC's apparent lack of impartiality, this does seem to be the case. The language choices of individual journalists can exert real power, as you have seen in this chapter, but the power of news institutions and organisations is huge. What they choose to cover – or refuse to cover – and the editorial angle they promote can be just as powerful, perhaps more so.

> **RESEARCH QUESTION**
> **Exploring impartiality**
>
> Research whether a nationwide broadcaster of your choice is impartial. You could find examples of specific complaints, analyse the language used in the original text and draw your own conclusion about bias and impartiality.
>
> You could also research the language of journalistic blogs, which can make a good topic for a language investigation. To research the language, you could:
>
> - choose a topic which is being reported widely by the media and compare how it is presented by a journalist writing for a national newspaper and by another writing their own blog
>
> - choose a controlled number of blogs from various journalists and explore the language they use, looking for common patterns across all the texts.

3.3 The language and power of advertising

So far you have seen that journalists can make specific language choices in order to manipulate and influence their readers and you will have formed an opinion on whether this fulfils their role or not. As you move on to look at advertising, you will see that its role is clear – to influence the receiver. Influential power, as introduced in Chapter 2, is one of the key features of advertising.

As with journalism, the number of platforms that carry adverts has expanded rapidly with the development of technology. For the purposes of this chapter, the focus will be on print advertising.

3.3.1 Reading advertisements

Thinking back to Hall's theory of audience positioning, the purpose of advertisements is to persuade. The approaches and therefore the language and graphology they use to achieve this can be very different. In this section, you will consider a range of different approaches:

- complimenting consumers
- appealing to elite consumers
- appealing to patriotic consumers
- appealing to consumers who don't want to be left out
- appealing to shocked consumers.

(In addition, you will then go on in Section 3.4 to consider an approach often used in charity appeals that is directed at emotional consumers.)

The way an audience is addressed makes an important contribution to audience positioning, so you will also start to analyse the language and graphology used, and the way these features exert power and influence. An audience may be addressed in different ways. It may be addressed directly to give information. It may be addressed in an authoritative manner or, in contrast, the producer may decide to address the audience in a familiar manner.

3.3.2 Complimenting consumers

To achieve a dominant reading, some advertisers use language to compliment the consumer or make them feel better about themselves. This is often done through the use of direct address, using the second-person pronoun 'you' to 'talk' directly to the consumer. L'Oréal's 'Because you're worth it' is probably one of the most famous examples and is representative of the way the beauty industry is one of the main users of compliments.

Take a close look at Text 3C, an advert from Elizabeth Arden. The sentence 'Clinically proven to take up to 10 years off the look of your skin' uses the second person possessive determiner 'your' to tell the consumer that they will benefit from the product and have better skin. Furthermore, the references to age reinforce the message that this product will make women feel better about themselves: 'ten years younger', 'capsule of youth', 'youth restoring'.

3 Language and Power

Text 3C

3.3.3 Appealing to elite consumers

Some companies want their customers to feel unique and special because they have a product not many other people possess. The car manufacturer Porsche is one such company, and has built several advertising campaigns on making their customers feel exclusive.

> **ACTIVITY 3.2**
> **Advertising exclusivity**
>
> Read the following statements, all taken from Porsche adverts. How do the advertisers use language to make their readers feel unique and part of an elite group?
>
> - You may get lost. But not in the crowd.
> - Don't listen to anyone who says you can't have a Porsche.
> - Your mother would be proud. Your father, jealous.
> - Absolutely wrong for so, so many people.

Language, power and the media

3.3.4 Appealing to patriotic consumers

Other advertisers try to appeal to the patriotic nature of their readers by making them feel proud of their country and persuading them that they will be patriotic if they buy a particular product or do what is being suggested.

Some of the most patriotic campaigns are linked to defending a country and urging people to join the armed forces. Such advertisements have a long history, from the recruitment posters of World War I to more modern advertisements to enlist. Patriotic advertising sometimes tries to make readers feel guilty and that they *must* act. Some adverts focus more on an assumed love of country. As an example, look at the language used in Texts 3D and 3E.

Text 3D

3 Language and Power

Text 3E

Advertisements that try to appeal to patriotic customers are excellent examples of influential power (see Chapter 2). Both Texts 3D and 3E, for example, use the second-person pronoun 'you' to directly address the audience. Other language features common to influential power texts include the following.

- **Interrogatives:** In Text 3D, the pragmatics of the question 'Daddy, what did YOU do in the Great War?' are that any father would want to say proudly that they fought in the war. The underlying message is that if a man doesn't enlist, he will regret it and be a disappointment to his children. In Text 3E, the interrogative uses the metaphor 'Star-Spangled heart', which evokes the American national anthem and a sense of national pride.

- **Imperatives:** In Text 3E, 'Join the WAC now!' is not mitigated in any way and acts an instruction that the audience is expected to follow.

- **Informal terms of address:** In Text 3D, the use of 'Daddy' is likely to have an emotional impact on the audience as it reinforces the idea that a father who does not enlist would be letting down his children. In Text 3E, the choice of 'girl' could be seen as rather informal and therefore creating a pseudo-relationship with the audience.

Given the cultural and historical context of these posters, it is likely that most of the target audience would share the producers' standpoint and their judgement of what is the right thing to do. The audience positioning reflects this. This in turn reflects the interdisciplinary approach of Critical Discourse Analysis (CDA) introduced in Chapter 2. Both production and consumption are important factors when analysing texts.

Patriotic advertising is not restricted to signing up to the army or fighting for your country. Some advertisers use patriotism to sell a range of different products, as shown in Table 3.3. Notice how the proper noun is used in each example to reinforce the patriotic ideal.

Table 3.3: Patriotism in advertising

Country	Product	Patriotic language
Australia	Protein bar	Keep <u>Australia</u> Beautiful
America	Alcohol	Made in <u>America</u> because that's how <u>America</u> was made
India	Banking	Proud to be <u>Indian</u>
Canada	McDonald's	World Famous Fries? Not without <u>Canadian</u> potato farmers

3.3.5 Appealing to customers who don't want to be left out

Some advertisements play on the receiver's natural feeling of wanting to be part of something or not wanting to be left out. They can be designed to make the consumer feel almost like an outcast if they don't use or buy a particular product. They can use various techniques to achieve this.

- Using a pronoun such as 'everyone' rather than 'you' in order to make the consumer feel they could be missing out: for example, 'Everyone is enjoying it!'
- Using an interrogative to make the consumer feel they need to be part of something: 'Cool phones and great prices. Who's in?'
- Using an imperative to achieve the same aim: 'Join the digital music revolution!'
- Using statistics to reinforce the idea of being part of the majority: '9 out of 10 dentists said they would recommend it', '5 million customers can't be wrong'.

3 Language and Power

3.3.6 Appealing to shocked consumers

Some advertisers employ the shock factor. They may decide to scare the consumer, playing on natural fears of things such as death. As well as making specific language choice, they may decide to shock with the graphology, using graphic or upsetting images to achieve their purpose. In Texts 3F and 3G, it is clear that the imagery is a significant contributory factor – its use is designed to shock.

In the context of the dangers of speeding in Text 3F, the picture of a small child's shoe is incredibly emotive as it perhaps makes the audience think that this is all that is left behind. It is clearly emotive as the death of a young person would shock anyone. The repeated use of the first person 'I' reinforces the idea about death and adds another emotional dimension as it appears very personal: the 'I' is the child who has died. The repetition of the second person 'you' adds a further emotive element: one of guilt and the inability to ever forget what has happened. The pragmatics of the verb 'killed' emphasises how the driver is solely responsible for the child's death – it makes it seem like a deliberate act which was totally preventable.

Text 3F

Another campaign included a series of photographs showing children whose eyes have been replaced by screaming mouths. The images are certainly very disturbing and unsettling, as shown in Text 3G. They were used to give the message that a child may access information on the internet that will disturb and shock them. The images are used to reflect the pragmatics behind the interrogative 'Do you know…?'; that is to say, if you don't know what your kids are watching, you are potentially causing them great harm. The informal word 'kids' adds another emotional layer with its connotations of innocence.

Text 3G

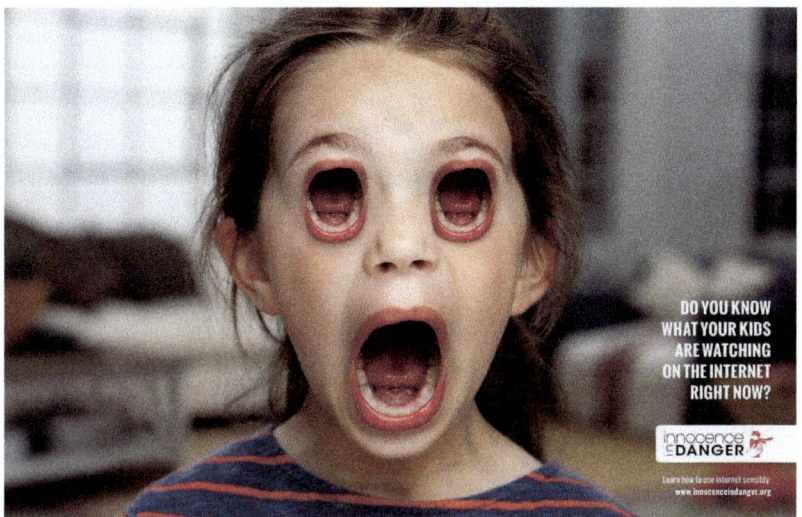

3.3.7 Using weasel words

As you have seen, various features are common to advertising in its aim to exert power and influence over audiences in the choice of graphology, modifiers, pronouns, imperatives, interrogatives and modal auxiliary verbs. Another common feature is the use of weasel words, which often include supposed facts and statistics.

> **KEY TERM**
>
> **Weasel words:** words or statements that are intentionally ambiguous or misleading (in folklore, weasels are often untrustworthy, easily adapting to situations in order to manipulate others)

Weasel words can be vague and ambiguous but make the consumer think the text is accurate and very meaningful. For example, an advert stating that a brand of chewing gum 'helps fight cavities' may make the consumer think that their dental hygiene will improve by using it. However, the words are actually very vague: 'helps fight' doesn't say how or by how much. Whilst the word 'fights' suggests strong action, the verb 'helps' suggests there are other factors involved and no medical evidence is given to prove that chewing gum stops cavities developing or enlarging. With the use of vague words and no medical claim, the advert cannot be proved to be making false claims.

Language and Power

Other weasel words include the following.

- 'Virtually': for example, 'Your kitchen will be virtually spotless'. Here, the consumer focuses on the modifier 'spotless' and makes the assumption that their kitchen will be ultra-clean. However, what does 'virtually' mean here? It can't actually be quantified.

- Comparatives such as 'better': for example, 'better than the rest'. The consumer is led to think a product is the best, beating all its competitors. But in what way is it better? There's no answer, casting doubt on the claim. Another example could be 'longer' as in 'it lasts longer'. Longer than what? Although the advert doesn't say, the consumer might still be persuaded to favour the product even though it not compared to anything specific.

- 'Up to': for example, 'kills up to 90% of germs'. The consumer will focus on the figure of 90% which seems a high percentage and therefore impressive. But what does 'up to' actually mean?

3.4 The language and power of charity appeals

Many of the features used in advertisements are also used by the producers of charity appeals. However, some charity appeals use a particular approach, which plays on the audience's emotions.

3.4.1 Appealing to emotional consumers

Charity appeals aim to make their audience feel sympathy for and empathy with their cause in order to gain support and financial contributions. To do this, they may try to make the receiver feel guilty, proud or confident, sad, jubilant or joyful.

Text 3H is the transcript of a WaterAid television appeal. It demonstrates power in discourse (see Chapter 2), as the language choices are certainly emotional. Furthermore, it also uses many of the features of influential power, as follows:

- Second-person pronoun: 'you can help save a child's life'

- Modifiers: 'dirty', 'stagnant'

- Noun phrases: 'dirty water deaths', 'clean water'

- Mitigated imperatives: 'please don't wait to save a child's life'

- Imperative: 'imagine your child…'

Language, power and the media

- Repetition: 'child', 'three pounds'
- Antithesis: 'dirty' and 'clean'
- Facts and statistics: 'in the next minute'
- Modal auxiliary verbs: 'will', 'can'.

Text 3H

> This is an appeal to **stop** dirty water deaths (.) **sadly** you won't see it in the news but today dirty water **will kill fourteen hundred children** more than malaria and AIDS combined (.) these children **have no choice** but to drink water from rivers swamps and stagnant ponds **every day** (.) imagine your child drinking dirty water knowing the next sip could kill them (1) right now **you can help** save a child's life (.) **simply text** tap to 70123 to give WaterAid three pounds (1) WaterAid **already has teams in place** to install the pipes pumps and taps (.) that **will bring** clean water to those children at risk (1) they just need your support (1) in the next minute dirty water **will kill** another child (.) so please (.) don't wait to save a child's life (.) text tap to 70123 to give three pounds now (.) **thank you** *[10 seconds showing an image of a young child with tears falling down their face with the caption Text TAP to 70123 to give £3 now on screen]*

ACTIVITY 3.3
Emotional language
Read Text 3H again and make notes on all the words and phrases in bold. Comment on how the language might make the receiver feel.

PRACTICE QUESTION
Using language to manipulate world views
Evaluate the idea that language can manipulate the ways in which different audiences see the world.

Wider reading

To develop your knowledge of the language used by journalists and advertisers, you could refer to and read the following:

The language of advertising

Cook, G. (1996) *The Discourse of Advertising* (Second edition). London: Routledge.

Goddard, A. (2002) *The Language of Advertising: Written Texts*. London: Routledge.

Ringrow, H. (2016) *The Language of Cosmetics Advertising*. London: Macmillan.

The language of journalism

Cotter, C. (2010) *News Talk: Investigating the Language of Journalism*. Cambridge, Cambridge University Press.

Richardson, J. E. (2006). *Analysing Newspapers: An Approach from Critical Discourse Analysis*. London: Palgrave Macmillan.

Richardson, J. E. (ed), (2007) *Language and Journalism*; Oxon: Routledge.

Smith, A. and Higgins, M. (2013); *The Language of Journalism: A Multi-genre Perspective*. London: Bloomsbury.

Chapter 4
Language, power and occupation

In this chapter you will:

- Develop an understanding of the spoken and written language of occupation
- Analyse how people communicate in the workplace, using speech and writing
- Explore the impact of hierarchy within organisations on language

4 Language and Power

4.1 Exclusive features of occupational language

> **ACTIVITY 4.1**
> **Reflecting on your own experiences**
> If you have worked part-time, think about the language you used at work. Discuss:
>
> - any specialised terminology you had to learn and why that was essential
> - ways in which colleagues addressed each other
> - any training you received in terms of how you should talk to customers/clients.

By reflecting on your own experiences, you have already begun thinking about how the workplace can influence language use. Research has shown that almost every occupation has its own special lexicon – a vocabulary that is specific to the occupation. This occurs in spoken and written modes. Some aspects of occupational language can be influenced by mode and whilst the specific language may differ from one occupation to another, there are common patterns. To build a picture of common discourse features, this section starts by exploring some of these key patterns – acronyms, jargon and codes – and then explains their use.

> **KEY TERM**
>
> **Lexicon:** the words used in a language or by a person or group of people

4.1.1 Acronyms

Organisations across the world are referred to by well-known acronyms: NHS in England (National Health Service), BMW worldwide (Bayerische Motoren Werke), CBS in America (Columbia Broadcasting System) and AENA in Spain (Aeropuertos Españoles y Aeronavegación Aérea). Whilst everyone may not be familiar with what these acronyms stand for, they are likely to recognise some of them and associate them with a particular business or type of organisation. However, occupational acronyms used within organisations will be far less

Language, power and occupation

understandable to outsiders and can therefore be regarded as part of a special lexicon.

Think about an occupation you have experience of – teaching. You may think you are familiar with 'teacher talk' but how many of the following acronyms do you know: AST, APP, AFL, CLA, CPD, EBD, ECM, FFT, FSM, IEP, NEET, PP? These particular acronyms are likely to be specific to the British education system so don't simply exclude non-teachers but also fellow professionals from other countries. Similarly, some of the acronyms listed on the Australian government's education website (www.cambridge.org/links/escpow6007) will be alien to British teachers:

- ASL: Aboriginal Student Liaison Officer
- NAPLAN: National Assessment Program in Literacy And Numeracy
- EDNA: Education Network Australia
- RAM funding: Resource Allocation Model (for education funding).

Acronyms are one form of specialised language used in many occupations. On the Metropolitan Police's website (www.cambridge.org/links/escpow6008) there is a glossary section for all the acronyms used by the police. The list is extensive; there are 61 entries under 'A' alone. These include some you may be familiar with (e.g. 'A&E' for 'Accident and Emergency') and many you are unlikely to understand (e.g. 'ASU' for 'Air Support Unit'). Other websites from across the world contain similar glossary pages. You could visit some of these to further understand how exclusive the use of acronyms can be:

- www.cambridge.org/links/escpow6009
- www.cambridge.org/links/escpow6010
- www.cambridge.org/links/escpow6011

It is such exclusivity that makes acronyms powerful. They create a discourse community. Those who use and understand the acronyms may feel powerful as they have knowledge others do not have.

KEY TERM

Discourse community: a group of people with shared interests and belief systems who are likely to respond to texts in similar ways

4 Language and Power

4.1.2 Jargon

Another way in which occupational language can instil a sense of exclusivity is in the use of jargon.

> **KEY TERM**
>
> **Jargon:** the vocabulary and manner of speech that define and reflect a particular profession but are difficult for others to understand

Recruits in the US Navy, for example, need to learn a fair amount of jargon. You may know or be able to guess the meaning of terms like: 'chow hall' (dining area), 'deck' (floor), 'jarhead' (a Marine), 'ladderwell' (stairs) and 'skivvies' (underwear). You may struggle with others: 'rainlocker' (shower), 'salty' (experienced), 'maggot' (sleeping bag), 'banjo' (sandwich), 'rollers' (hot dogs).

Another familiar source of jargon is the local supermarket. On a recent visit the author made to one particular store, a tannoy announcement asked 'Could all team leaders report for today's 4 o'clock rumble'. Whilst you can probably guess from the context that a 'rumble' is some form of meeting, its purpose is less obvious and it is possible that its use in this way is unique to this company. In the section headed 'How do we communicate with each other?', the staff handbook for another supermarket includes various phrases that are unlikely to be understood by non-employees. According to the handbook, communication in this company is achieved through 'Team5', 'SQTs', 'Protector Line' and 'Steering Wheel'. It is unlikely that these phrases are used by other companies; they appear unique to this particular employer and create a shared knowledge and understanding amongst employees.

Some jargon can be linked to roles or jobs within specific industries. You may recognise the various roles, or job titles, within police forces. In the UK, there are titles such as Detective Inspector, Police Constable and Superintendent, whilst in Australia the ranks include First Constable, Senior Constable and Commander. However, roles/jobs in other industries may be less easy to understand. In the UK mining industry, for example, the following job titles were used and, most likely, only understood by workers and the mining community.

- A 'checkweighman' was paid for by the miners themselves to check the records of the man who weighed the coal as it was taken out of the mine.

- A 'hewer' was someone who cut the coal.

- A 'putter' used to bring empty tubs up to the workers at the coal face and take loaded tubs to the pit bottom.

- A 'shaftsinker' was employed to sink the shafts of a new mine. He usually migrated to new coalfields as these were developed.
- A 'trapper' was a child employed to open and close the door in a roadway through which coal was brought (www.cambridge.org/links/escpow6012).

4.1.3 Codes

The use of codes within certain jobs is a further feature of occupational language. All retail and hospitality outlets, for example, use coded tannoy announcements which, it is expected, will only be understood by staff. These coded messages can be quite clear ('This is a staff announcement. We have a code 3') or less obvious by using a name to signify a situation ('Can Mr Stack please report to the manager's office').

Codes to signify a specific situation are also used extensively by the emergency services. The British police, for example, use codes to describe people of different origins. IC1 is the code for a white person whilst IC5 is used when referring to a Chinese, Japanese or South-East Asian person. The American police also use codes to refer to a particular crime, for example 215 refers to carjacking, 211 is used for a robbery and 586 for illegal parking.

Coded language relies on exclusive shared knowledge and understanding, and the link to discourse communities is very clear.

4.1.4 The power of exclusive language

One of the reasons why professional organisations may develop their own vocabulary is to be part of a discourse community. This choice of language gives employers a form of status – they can use and understand language which 'outsiders' cannot. They are the experts.

Janet Holmes and Maria Stubbe (2003) discuss the similar idea of 'communities of practice', a concept which was developed by Jean Lave and Etienne Wenger (Lave and Wenger 1991; Wenger 2000). Holmes and Stubbe define it as 'groups who regularly engage with each other in the service of a joint enterprise and who share a repertoire of resources which enables them to communicate in a kind of verbal shorthand which is often difficult for outsiders to penetrate'. It could be argued that through use of jargon (as well as acronyms and codes) occupational groups form one of these communities of practice.

Penelope Eckert (2006) recognises the importance of language use in such communities. She argues that, 'It provides an accountable link between the individual, the group, and place in the broader social order, and it provides a setting in which linguistic practice emerges as a function of this link'. The use of

4 Language and Power

an exclusive vocabulary creates a sense of identity for all those involved. Bernard Spolsky (1998) says that 'A specialised jargon serves not just to label new and needed concepts, but to establish bonds between members of the in-group and enforce boundaries for outsiders. If you cannot understand my jargon, you don't belong to my group'. Andrzej Kollataj (2009) argues that using such jargon is not stigmatised when compared to other language choices (for example, slang) that mark group boundaries. Thus it is accepted as a form of language; such acceptance makes it powerful.

ACTIVITY 4.2
Exploring language used for precision

There may be other reasons behind language choices within a given occupation or industry. One such reason may be the need for precision and to avoid any confusion. In these two definitions, consider how the precision helps avoid ambiguity and makes the differences in the offences very clear:

- Aggravated burglary: entering premises armed with a weapon, intending to steal goods.
- Burglary: entering a building without permission with the intention of stealing or doing damage.

With this example in mind:

- Which other professions are more likely to use exclusive language or jargon for precision?
- What are the benefits of using exclusive language or jargon for precision?

4.2 Workplace interactions

Interaction within the workplace occurs in different contexts, both formally and informally. One of the most common formal contexts is meetings. Holmes (2009a) cites research which indicates 'that meetings occupy anything between 25% and 80% of work time'. As they are such an integral part of many people's working days, it is perhaps unsurprising that there has been a great deal of research into the way language is used in workplace meetings.

4.2.1 Roles and hierarchy in workplace meetings

Within any meeting, it is likely that the participants have different roles and that there is a hierarchical structure in place. At the top of this hierarchy is the chairperson, who runs the meeting and has personal power. Due to their status and authority, you might expect the chairperson to hold the floor, initiate topics, ask questions and control who speaks. This can happen, as shown in research from Holmes (2009b), who reported how one chairperson, 'Kenneth', had an authoritative leadership style; this was reflected in his structured and controlling way of chairing meetings. The agenda was followed closely and he took an active role in controlling the talk by allocating speaking turns to his colleagues. There was a focus on individual accountability. Colleagues addressed their responses to him; they knew they were accountable to him in the meeting.

However, chairpersons do not always take on such an authoritative role. Instead, some act more as a facilitator in a meeting. In the same piece of research from Holmes (2009b), the meeting management style of 'Tricia' was also explored. 'Tricia' took on a facilitator role, encouraging team members to participate in discussions and bring up topics of their own – she was not as rigid with the content of the meetings as 'Kenneth'. Furthermore, she encouraged social talk and humour during her meetings. She took on a more empowering leadership style, recognising and encouraging the importance of collaboration, consultation and cooperation. That is not to say that 'Tricia' was herself lacking in power and authority. She was leading this type of meeting; it was her conscious decision to run meetings in this way. She was still in charge, directing how the meetings ran.

Read Text 4A, a transcript in which it is clear that Pam, the chairperson, is taking on a role much more like 'Tricia'.

Text 4A

Pam:	okay (.) what we got on the agenda for today (.) who wants to go first (.)
Mark:	well Kate's two items are still left over from last week
Kate:	yeah I don't mind I'll do my bits first (.) I just wanted to check first of all what we were (.) what the plan is for replacing Tony
Joe:	I think it's part of a bigger discussion we need to have (.) to think about staffing (.) I don't know what you think Mark
Mark:	yeah (.) there's lots to discuss and look at (.) there might be others leaving (.) we might need to hang on for a bit longer (.) you know to (.) see the whole (.) the bigger picture (.) and look at what we need

4 Language and Power

Pam:	yeah I think that's the best way forward (.) there's no point in making plans which we might have to change anyway (.) that's what I'm thinking anyway (.) don't know about anyone else
Kate:	yeah I was thinking the same (.) I wasn't meaning (.) I wasn't thinking we sort it now (.) I just wanted to check the plans
Joe:	do we know if anyone else is making noises about leaving this year
Mark:	not that that I know of
Pam:	no one has been to me so I don't think so (.) unless anyone else has heard anything

In this transcript, Pam's use of the discourse marker 'okay' to start the meeting signals she is in charge and ready to begin. However, she doesn't dictate the agenda and rather invites one of her colleagues to take the floor through her use of the interrogative 'who wants to go first'. What follows is a discussion between the other colleagues, in which they encourage each other to participate in the meeting (for example, when Joe nominates Mark to speak). Pam becomes involved on a similar level to the others. Her utterances after the initial introduction to the meeting do not suggest she is trying to be authoritarian. When she gives her opinion or offers some information, she follows it up with a cue for others to respond and become involved: 'don't know about anyone else' and 'unless anyone else has heard anything'. She opens this up to the whole group rather than allocating a speaking turn to an individual as 'Kenneth' had done in Holmes' study.

However, in Text 4B, Pam is leading a different meeting in which the results are not similar at all. In this transcript, she is leading a meeting with a larger group of staff.

Text 4B

Pam:	morning everyone (.) hope everyone had a great break (.) welcome back (.) year 7 (2) Alex
Alex:	just to let everyone know we've got a new starter this morning (.) the family have moved into the area (.) I've emailed all his teachers but any issues just let me know
Pam:	thanks Alex (.) any more year 7 (2) year 8 (1) Tim
Tim:	yeah (.) there are some year 8s who want to do a (.) something extra for Children in Need (.) so they've organised a bake sale (.) they'll be selling cakes and stuff at break and lunch outside the Maths block (.) if we can pop along and see (.) support them that'd be brill (.) thanks

Pam:	that's great Tim (.) I'll definitely be there (.) year 9 (3) no (.) ok year 10 (1) yes Laura
Laura:	this is for 10 and 11 (.) can tutors please remind their tutor groups that there's a D of E meeting today at break in S5 (.) thanks

In this transcript, Pam is clearly following a set structure and does so rigidly. She leads the discourse and invites other colleagues to speak by name ('Yes Laura'). There is no negotiation of roles here – Pam is in control and the other staff respond only when appropriate.

The difference between the two transcripts could perhaps lead to the conclusion that the most influential factor is not the personality or authority of a specific person or the authority of the role of chairperson. Instead the most influential factor could be the context, the purpose of the meeting and the participants involved. In the first transcript, Pam is in a meeting with six colleagues who are all part of a small team of equals. In the second transcript, Pam is talking to the whole staff in a far shorter meeting in which the sole purpose is to share key information. In this latter context, the more authoritarian manner is most appropriate.

RESEARCH QUESTION
Chairing a meeting

There is further research on the different ways someone in authority will chair a meeting. Some research supports the findings from 'Tricia', whilst other findings are more in line with what Holmes concluded about 'Kenneth'.

Investigate the following research, exploring what conclusions are drawn and how they support each of the management styles that Holmes discovered:

- Barnes, R. (2007) 'Formulations and the facilitation of common agreement in *meetings* talk', *Text & Talk*, 27 (3).

- Kangasharju, H. and Nikko, T. (2009) 'Emotions in Organizations: Joint Laughter in Workplace Meetings'. Available at: www.cambridge.org/links/escpow6014

- Pomerantz, A. and Denvir, P. (2007). In F. Cooren (ed.) *Interacting and Organizing: Analyses of a Management Meeting*. London: L. Erlbaum.

4 Language and Power

> - Sandlund, E. and Denk, T. (2007). In B. Asmuß and J. Svennevig, *Meeting Talk*. Available at: www.cambridge.org/links/escpow6013
> - Svennevig, J. (2008 and 2011) 'Interaction in workplace meetings'. Available at: www.cambridge.org/links/escpow6015
>
> If you need to carry out your own research as part of your studies, you may wish to use these various theories as a starting point. You could then record and transcribe a meeting and draw your own conclusions as to the role of the chairperson. You could, for example, attend a student council meeting.

4.3 The negotiation of roles: the customer is always right

Another important context of language in the workplace is in the relationship between supplier (company employee) and customer or client. There are many industries in which the customer is involved in interaction within the workplace. This may be face-to-face or could be via technology such as email or telephone. As a worker in such industries, training is always given in how to speak to and treat customers in a respectful manner. In service industries, this leads to the question: Who exactly is in power – the customer or the worker?

Read Text 4C, the transcription of an interaction between a customer and a call centre worker.

Text 4C

Staff:	good morning (.) this is Maria speaking how can I help you today	
Customer:	erm (.) hi I was just I was wanting to cancel my membership my account please	
Staff:	no problem Sir (.) can I please take your post code	
Customer:	yeah (.) it's W F twenty two nine double A	
Staff:	thank you (.) can I also take your membership number please	
Customer:	yeah (.) it's six one zero nine	
Staff:	thank you (2) so that is Mr Joe Benson	

Language, power and occupation

Customer:	yeah that's right
Staff:	thank you (.) do you have any objection to me using your first name today
Customer:	no no that's fine
Staff:	thank you Joe (.) I see from our records Joe that you have been a customer for several years now (.) can I ask why you wish to close your account
Customer:	it's just er just that I don't use it enough to be honest so it's like a waste of money to be honest
Staff:	I understand that Joe (.) but before I close your account what I can do for you today is inform you of a very special offer due to your loyalty with us (.) does that sound like something you would be interested in Joe
Customer:	no I'm fine thanks I just wanna just want to cancel my account thanks
Staff:	yes I understand Joe (.) does a saving of sixty pounds not interest you
Customer:	thanks anyway but I'm fine
Staff:	I am sorry you are leaving us but what I will do for you is cancel your account with immediate effect and recall today's payment (5) thank you for your patience Joe (.) your account is now cancelled
Customer:	thanks very much
Staff:	thank you for calling Joe and you have a good day
Customer:	yes you too (.) bye

In this transcript, it could be argued that the member of staff has the power as she leads the conversation through question and answer adjacency pairs. It is likely this is something she has been trained to do and she may even be reading from a script. However, the customer also has power as he is dictating the outcome of the conversation. He has a clear goal which, despite some attempts to change the final outcome, is achieved.

KEY TERM
Adjacency pair: a simple structure of two turns

4 Language and Power

In his study of the language of outsourced call centres, Eric Friginal (2009) researched the discourse in calls between a Philippines-based call centre serving American customers. Friginal found some common patterns in the language of members of staff:

- use of second-person pronoun
- use of the imperative 'let's'
- use of brand names and other related proper nouns
- use of the present tense
- use of specialised, technical terms
- use of politeness markers
- use of discourse markers
- fewer topic shifts than an everyday conversation
- limited use of hedges and vague language.

> **KEY TERM**
>
> **Hedges:** words or phrases which soften what is said or written to make it less direct

When looking at the language of the customer, he also found common characteristics in the use of:

- first-person pronouns
- past tense
- interrogatives and words such as 'what' and 'why'
- informal lexis
- short responses.

From these lists, it appears that members of staff used more features of powerful language. However, they do give some power to customers through, for example, their use of politeness markers and terms of address such as 'Mr…', 'sir', 'ma'am'.

Language, power and occupation

> **PRACTICE QUESTION**
> **Who has the power?**
> Referring to Text 4C and Friginal's study, how do members of staff and customers show power? Identify key linguistic features and evaluate their success in creating or establishing power.

Wider reading

To gain a wider understanding of how language is used in the workplace and how this is linked to power, you could refer to the following books:

Dent, S. (2016) *Modern Tribes*. London: John Murray Publishers.

Friginal, E. (2009) *The Language of Outsourced Call Centers: A Corpus-Based Study of Cross-Cultural Interaction.* Philadelphia, PA: John Benjamins Publishing.

Holmes, J. (2006) *Gendered Talk at Work*. London: Blackwell.

Holmes, J. and Stubbe, M. (2003) *Power and Politeness in the Workplace: A Sociolinguistic Analysis of Talk at Work.* Abingdon: Routledge.

Chapter 5
Language, power and education

In this chapter you will:

- Explore how language is used in the practice of teaching
- Consider the link between language and the role of teachers
- Analyse how language is used to create power in the classroom

Language, power and education

This chapter explores how language is used in an education context and how the various hierarchies within that context are reinforced through language. There are two distinct elements that could be considered here: classroom discourse, and wider practices and procedures in the education context. The focus in this chapter will be on the classroom, looking at the roles played by teachers and students in this context.

5.1 Traditional classroom discourse

Society accepts the asymmetrical relationship between teacher and student, and that the teacher is the powerful person due to their role and status. In Chapter 2 you learned that this acceptance gives the teacher instrumental power.

5.1.1 How teachers demonstrate instrumental power

Within the classroom, a teacher may show their power in a number of ways. They may:

- direct and instruct students
- gain the attention of students
- challenge students
- dictate how and when students speak.

To begin thinking about how teachers use language in these ways, study Text 5A, a transcript from a Year 7 English lesson (11–12-year-old students) in the UK. Think about the ways the teacher uses language to show her power.

Text 5A

T: right then (.) listen up (.) you've got your notes (.) page notes (.) right (.) Will (.) can you leave the table alone (.) thank you (1) right (.) before you do your talks I'm going to show you an example of a bad talk (.) and I'm going to give you (.) give each of you a post it note and what I want you to do is to write down (.) on that post it note (.) a target for the person doing the talk (1) right (1) so (.) I'll give you a post it note erm to write a target for the person giving the talk (.) you look a bit down (.) you alright (1)

P1: miss the bottom's come off of my shoe

T: oh erm (.) we'll find someone to sort that out for you (.) no worries (.) sure there is someone in the technology block who has some glue (.)

5 Language and Power

> ok (.) hands down everyone (.) wait until I've told everyone (.) told you all what we're up (.) going to do today (2) Adam why's your hand up
>
> P2: miss I got a trophy this morning
>
> T: what did you get your trophy for (.) oh tell you what you can tell me more about that later on (.) did I give you guys a post it (.) can you talk to me (.) what's the face for Ricky (.) nobody wants to do it at first but everyone when they've done it feels great (.) Ok (.) Ok (.) ready (.) so (.) pick your target for this person in an example of a bad talk (.) don't start chatting guys (.) Josh (2) thank you

Directing and instructing the students

To do this, the teacher uses an interrogative and an imperative.

- At the start of the transcript, the teacher uses the interrogative 'can you leave the table alone', despite not actually meaning it as a question. Pragmatically this is an instruction with the expectation that the student sees it as an order and complies. This expectation is reinforced when the teacher immediately follows the interrogative with the politeness marker 'thank you', rather than with the more common politeness marker 'please'. There is an assumption that the table will be left alone. The teacher uses this technique to ensure that her instructions are carried out.

- She also uses an imperative to direct and instruct: 'pick your target…'. Imperatives are common features of instrumental power, as discussed in Chapter 2, and act as a clear indicator of someone's role and status. A teacher's role gives them the authority to give direct orders and this authority is accepted in the classroom context. In this case, the imperative is task based with the desired outcome of the students producing some work. As you will see, this is just one reason for using an imperative.

Gaining the attention of the students

To ensure the students are paying attention to her, the teacher uses discourse markers, an imperative and students' names.

- In this transcript, discourse markers are the key tool the teacher uses to get the students' attention. She uses 'right', 'ok' and 'so' in an attempt to focus the students on what she is saying. This is a common technique used by speakers in spontaneous speech and not necessarily used as a power tool. Often discourse markers are used to signpost discourse, inviting turn-taking or joining ideas together. On occasions, they are also used in a more controlling manner, as in this transcript. They act as a signal to the students that they need to focus on the teacher or that they need to listen to what follows.

Language, power and education

- The teacher also uses an imperative to gain attention when she says 'listen up', demonstrating another function of imperatives in teacher/student discourse.
- She also uses students' names to gain attention: 'Will (.) can you…'; 'what's the face for Ricky'. This is a common classroom technique and an obvious one when the discourse may involve 30 different people. The need to direct a question or statement at an individual by using their name is, of course, necessary in the context. Using someone's name during a one-to-one conversation is far less likely.

> **KEY TERM**
>
> **Discourse marker:** a word, phrase or clause that helps to organise what is said or written (e.g. 'OK', 'so', 'as I was saying…')

Challenging students

One inherent, and accepted, aspect of a teacher's role is to challenge any actions by students that are inappropriate given the context, and to then reinforce rules and expectations. This power is linked to the accepted hierarchy within the classroom; the teacher has power behind the discourse and, according to Wareing, personal power (as discussed in Chapter 2). In Text 5A, the teacher challenges the students by using an interrogative and an imperative.

- After giving the instruction 'hands down…', she uses the interrogative 'Adam why's your hand up' to challenge him for not following instructions. Here again it could be argued that the teacher does not really want an answer; instead she wants Adam to put his hand down and thus follow the initial instruction.
- The teacher also uses the imperative 'don't start chatting guys' which acts as a direct challenge to the students' actions. There is a clear purpose here – that the students modify their behaviour. Once again, due to the teacher's personal power and status within the school context, this expectation is likely to be met. However, it could be argued that this particular teacher softens and mitigates the imperative by using the informal term 'guys' at the end. This may be a further attempt by the teacher to develop the relationship to ensure the students act as she wants them to.

Dictating how and when students speak

Teachers may also influence speaking rights; that is to say they might decide which students may speak and when during a lesson. In many classroom interactions, the teacher will hold the floor and control the discourse, as you saw in Chapter 2. It is accepted that teachers can speak as much as they want and say whatever they want in the classroom whilst students are far more restricted and need permission to speak. In Text 5A, students are invited to speak through

5 Language and Power

the use of an interrogative which invites a response: 'you alright'. In many cases this will be linked to teacher nomination, when the teacher decides who to question. The question/answer discourse structure is very common in classrooms and often followed by an evaluation or feedback, often referred to as initiate, respond, evaluation/feedback (IRE or IRF), as in Text 5B.

Text 5B

> T: what punctuation mark should we use here
>
> P: a comma
>
> T: excellent (.) well done

> **KEY TERM**
>
> **Initiation, Response, Evaluation/Feedback (IRE/IRF):** three-part conversational exchange in which a speaker starts the conversation, a second speaker responds and the first speaker then provides some feedback to what the second speaker said

The use of IRE/IRF has been the subject of research, with the work of John Sinclair and Malcolm Coulthard (1975) being particularly influential. According to Sinclair and Coulthard, the discourse in a classroom is rather rigid and led by the teacher. It is the teacher's role to initiate the exchange (often through questions) and then, once the student has responded, to offer some evaluative comment. The student expects some feedback; they want to know if they are right or wrong so that they are developing their knowledge and understanding. They may also be seeking praise from the teacher for being an active participant in the exchange. Thus the IRE/IRF structure relates once again to the concept of role as the teacher is the one with the accepted status and authority.

The idea of speaking rights certainly links to the asymmetrical relationship in a classroom but the IRF model also points to the need for teachers to be positive, supportive and encouraging of their students. This can also be achieved through what O'Connor and Michaels (1996) termed 'revoicing', when teachers include the student's response in the subsequent discourse. O'Connor and Michaels claimed that repeating what the student says serves various purposes:

- to draw other students' attention to the comment and show its importance
- to encourage better understanding whilst still recognising and sharing the importance of the contribution
- to encourage further discussion and contribution (similar to IRE/IRF).

Language, power and education

The actual questions teachers use are another important aspect of how they dictate how and when students speak. Mary Budd Rowe has made this aspect of classroom discourse a major focus of her research. She argues that 'when teachers ask questions of students, they typically wait 1 second or less for the students to start a reply; after the student stops speaking they begin their reaction or proffer the next question in less than 1 second'. However, if the teacher waits longer (for example, three seconds or more) 'there are pronounced changes in student use of language as well as in student and teacher attitudes and expectations' (Rowe 1986). This idea of 'wait time' has become a well-known teaching technique and Rowe's research showed that by using it teachers ask fewer questions but that more questions are complex. Furthermore, she found that teachers become more adept at responding to students' contributions and that their expectations of students increase, resulting in less passive learning and more active participants. In relation to power in the classroom, Rowe's research shows that the teacher is dictating the discourse by introducing 'wait time' when questioning students.

The key language features and concepts used by teachers that have been discussed so far are summarised in Figure 5.1.

Figure 5.1: Key language features and concepts used by teachers

The language of teachers:
- Interrogatives
- Imperatives
- Use of a student's name
- Politeness markers
- Discourse markers
- IRF discourse structure
- Revoicing
- Wait time

69

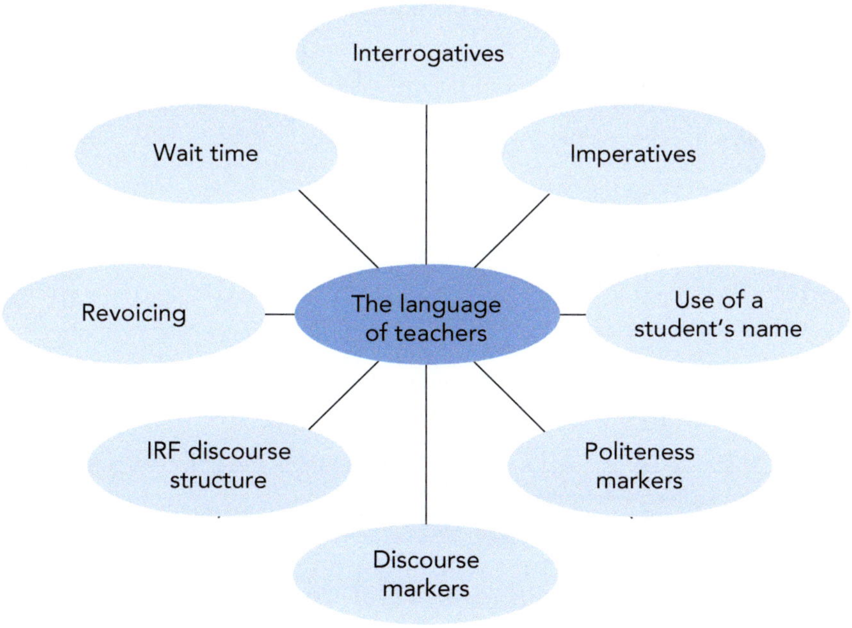

5 Language and Power

ACTIVITY 5.1
Exploring key features of teacher/student talk

Read Texts 5C and 5D, both transcripts of teacher/student talk. Then annotate the transcripts, identifying as many of the key language features shown in Figure 5.1 as you can. Can you find examples of each feature? Can you identify common patterns? Are there other language features which are common across the transcripts?

Once you have annotated the data, discuss why the teachers might have used specific language features. Can you, for example, see how imperatives may have different functions?

Text 5C

T: so my first activity for you guys is this (.) you can do it in a four (.) I want you to look at these different kinds of contextual thingamajigs (.) right (.) I want you to put them into like (.) a pyramid (.) so what you think is the most important (.) at the top and kind of (2) what's next most important and make it into a pyramid (.) alright with that (2) separate them first of all and then you can talk to each other (.) Elle alright

P1: yeah miss (.)

T: so what do you think might be at the top

P1: erm (.) I was thinking when it were written

T: yes when it was written that's definitely important (.) any other ideas (2) Ryan

P2: could audience be up there

T: audience (.) yes I think it would up there (.) but why do you think that's important

P2: because I guess if like (.) the author (.) I think the author would have an audience in mind

Language, power and education

Text 5D

T: okay everyone (.) coats off quickly (.) let's get settled (.) Michael (.) thank you (2) Zoe (3) Zoe I'm waiting (.) that's better (.) right year 9 everyone looking this way (.) Anne (.) let's all think back to last lesson (.) who can remember how we make sure it is carbon dioxide (.) remember it could be anything couldn't it (.) how can we make sure it is carbon dioxide people (3) okay (.) what's the test for carbon dioxide (2) Michael

P1: a glowing splint

T: a glowing splint no that's not the one (2) well done for having a go Michael (.) come on you lot what does that test for (2) James

P2: hydrogen

T: not hydrogen (3) not hydrogen no

P3: oxygen

T: oxygen (.) what does it do to it Nicola

P3: relights the splint

T: relights the splint (.) well done (.) are you listening Jack (.) put that pen down so I can see you're paying attention (.) so what's the test for hydrogen then since someone brought that one up (.) Jack

P4: dunno

T: you don't know (.) have a try (.) you can have a go (.) it's something to do with a splint

5.2 A more collaborative classroom

So far in this chapter, the focus has been on teachers being in charge. It is teachers who steer and influence discourse. They ask the questions, students respond and teachers feed back. However, research has also shown that there is often a more collaborative approach to teaching. Dillon (1983) argued that discussions in a classroom are not always led by teacher questions. Instead he found that teachers also use declarative statements, offer reflective comments, invite other students to elaborate, or say nothing and use silence as a tool to encourage discussion. Thus the teacher almost becomes less authoritative in the students' minds and more of a facilitator in the discussion. Such techniques improve communication and are an attempt to get the most reticent of learners to become more involved. Such discussion stimulates deeper thinking rather than a closed question/answer session. Consider the speech bubbles around Figure 5.2 and how the teacher is encouraging more discussion amongst a group of students.

Figure 5.2: Encouraging collaboration

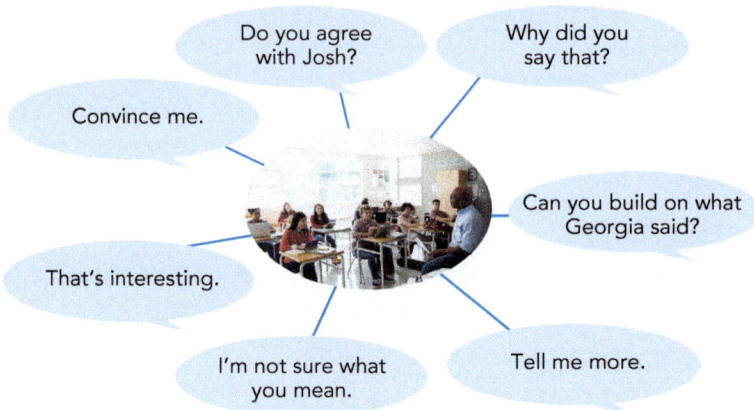

It is clear in each of these utterances that the teacher is not relying on the IRF structure or on asking closed questions. Instead, they are using their role and status to encourage wider contributions. At times the teacher will remove themselves from the discussion, encouraging students to question each other and communicate as a group. Jay Lemke (1982) discussed this idea, calling it 'cross-discussion': 'Cross-Discussion is dialogue between students in which teacher is not a constant intermediary. Such dialogue is rare as part of the discourse of the classroom … Public cross-discussion is signalled when one student addresses another publicly rather than addressing teacher [or] if teacher is referred to in the third person.' Therefore, the teacher relinquishes their role but it is important to remember that they have the authority to do this and, as they are still a presence in the discussion, their influence and power is still evident.

The collaborative classroom is certainly an emerging area in education. As the Center for the Collaborative Classroom in California, USA states, 'Teachers who use the Collaborative Classroom model make an intentional shift from having a classroom where they do the majority of the talking to constructing a learning situation and then facilitating it through student thinking and talking': (www.cambridge.org/links/escpow6016). This is clearly a departure from the more structured discourse which Sinclair and Coulthard presented in their research. However, it is important to recognise that the role of the teacher is vital to the success of a collaborative classroom. Students will not automatically be fully engaged in the shifting dynamics of such a classroom. Teachers need to know how to make it work, first teaching the principles to their students. They will need to:

- establish rules for group discussion
- teach students how to listen effectively

- demonstrate what good questioning looks like
- ensure certain students do not dominate
- teach students how to respond appropriately.

Therefore, the role of the teacher remains vital in this negotiation of roles to create a supportive learning environment.

> **ACTIVITY 5.2**
> Extended teacher talk
>
> Texts 5E and 5F are transcripts from the same lesson. Read the transcripts and consider the following questions.
>
> - In what ways does this teacher dominate the classroom?
> - What could the teacher change to facilitate a more collaborative classroom?

Text 5E

> Now we've got lots to do this morning, you're going to need to ignore what's going on behind me, ah, it's not happening, right, as I said to you at the very beginning of September I'm the star, so you pay attention to me. That was the correct thing to do, very well though, you saw the look and you decided. On the board this morning we're going to have a bash at thinking about some targets, we're going to have a bash think about, how you think you've done so far? One of the two tasks that I've set you since we met in September, what are the two big tasks that we've concentrated on? One should be in your file already and it should be finished and the other one you're going to give to me today.
>
> Taken from the Cambridge English Corpus

Text 5F

> Yes, the time when it has to come in, the day I say I want to collect it, now you might need to say to yourself, oh dear, Mrs deadline was, have I met it? No, or yes I'm mega brilliant, yes I did meet the deadline. Now I'm going to help you with it and what I suggest we do this morning when I give you these sheets will you please write your name and today's date at the top of the sheet and I put the date on the board, and then can you please resist the temptation to start, start writing over the rest of the sheet until I've gone through it with you. You can certainly have a read but please resist the

5 Language and Power

temptation to write on it. Right the sheets are coming round, when you get yours, your name on it and today's date on it please, that's all, I've already punched holes in it so it's ready to go in your file [pause] Now is there anyone who does not have one of these sheets, it says at the top year seven, module one, survey on belief. Is there anyone who does not have a copy in front of them? Please write your name and the date. The date is on the board [pause] Oh, we'll do that later that one, get you another one [pause] good, most people seem to of done that. […] Okay, let's start going down these six sections. Section one says, now for this everybody we're thinking about the survey you did in the form room, from which you did your graphs, saying to people do you believe in god, have you visited a place of worship, is everyone clear about the piece of work we're thinking about, speak to me.

Taken from the Cambridge English Corpus

It is clear that power in the classroom ultimately lies with the teacher. They are the ones who ask all the questions, give instructions, offer feedback, encourage participation, challenge students' attitudes and behaviour, direct who can speak and when, and ensure students' attention is focused on them. To do this they use a range of language features which are accepted and expected by the students in this context. However, it is also important to recognise that the distinct roles of teacher and student can become slightly blurred to further develop a student's thinking and learning.

Wider reading

You can find out more about the topics in this chapter by reading the following:

Cole, K. and Zuengler, J. (2017) *The Research Process in Classroom Discourse Analysis: Current Perspectives*. London: Routledge.

Moorman, C. and Moorman-Weber, N. (1989) *Teacher Talk: What It ReallyMeans*. Bay City, MI: Institute for Personal Power.

Rymes, B. (2015) *Classroom Discourse Analysis: A Tool For Critical Reflection*, (Second Edition). London: Routledge.

Walsh, S. (2013) *Classroom Discourse and Teacher Development*. Edinburgh: Edinburgh University Press.

Walsh, S. (2011) *Exploring Classroom Discourse: Language in Action*. Abingdon: Taylor & Francis.

Chapter 6
Language, power and politics

In this chapter you will:

- Reflect on some of the ways that political language can be used to influence, persuade, manipulate and coerce an audience

- Consider how the Critical Discourse Analysis model may be applied to political discourse

- Examine the use of rhetorical devices in political speeches, interviews and debates

6 Language and Power

6.1 Ideology and Critical Discourse Analysis

In his treatise about political language, writer and essayist George Orwell (1945: 20) levied this charge: '[it] is designed to make lies sound truthful and murder respectable, and to give an appearance of solidity to pure wind'. This may seem rather exaggerated, but many believe that political language is designed to manipulate and obscure truths. Language is perhaps one of the most important tools at a politician's disposal and it is through the skilful manipulation of language that politicians present their beliefs and goals to the electorate, aiming to influence people of the truth and legitimacy of their political stance.

There is a clear link between politics and ideology. Society is made up of two important apparatuses: government and administration, which establishes and maintains the rules and laws that people must adhere to, and ideology, a set of beliefs held by people within any given society. If people are to accept rules and laws, then they must accept and share in common ideologies. This may be done on both a conscious and subconscious level.

Marxist philosopher Louis Althusser (1970) stated that society is unequal and that this inequality is embedded into social structures through Ideological State Apparatuses (ISAs). Society is made up of many institutions such as education, family, religion and the media. Although these institutions are not part of state control, they are systems through which the values of the state are presented so that those values seem 'natural' and 'common sense'. Aligning ourselves with what is considered 'natural' means that we are more likely to accept mainstream ideologies, even if they conflict with what we might really think and believe.

6.1.1 CDA and presenting messages in political posters

Critical Discourse Analysis (see Chapter 2), is a useful way of exploring how political texts are shaped. Applying Fairclough's model can show how language features are used in texts to present particular messages and ideas. Texts can be taken at face value, but examining social and discourse practices helps readers recognise and engage with any underlying messages.

Take a look at the billboard poster in Text 6A, which was produced by one of the main political parties in the UK.

Language, power and politics

Text 6A

Conservative Party campaign poster, 1978

Although there is relatively minimal written language in this text, the words were carefully chosen to reflect a particular ideology.

'Labour isn't working'

- The word 'labour' can be interpreted in various ways:
  - as a common noun to denote 'work'
  - to denote a workforce
  - as a verb to imply physical effort and hard work
  - to refer to the Labour Party, a UK political party.
- The juxtaposition of 'labour' with 'working' forces the reader to question the relationship between the two words: a labour force usually works.
- The negative 'isn't' suggests that 'labour' is not functioning as it should, emphasised by the juxtaposition of 'labour' and 'work'.
- The image anchors the message: an exaggerated queue of people, typical of those waiting in line for the unemployment office.

'Britain's better off with the Conservatives'

- The use of the comparative 'better' is a positive term, suggesting an improved future.
- 'Better off' is a colloquial term, suggesting that the 'labour force' will be in a better financial position under a Conservative government.

6 Language and Power

- 'Britain' refers to the whole country's perceived gain under a Conservative government, creating a collective ideology.

A billboard poster needs to be simple and clear, with a strong message so that readers read and respond in the preferred way quickly. The poster was produced by the UK Conservative Party, which targeted its campaign directly against the Labour Party, foregrounding the opposition's inability to meet the needs of the electorate.

The text reflects key dominant ideologies which are considered 'natural' and common sense. In Western cultures, economic security is key – everyone wants the opportunity to work towards a better future and be financially rewarded for this work. No one wants to be at the back of a seemingly never ending queue. This poster promises a successful future under a Conservative government. Without it, Britain will be left with a society failing to work and succeed.

ACTIVITY 6.1
Applying the CDA model to political campaign posters

Texts 6B and 6C are taken from British political campaigns. What dominant ideologies are presented in each one? Which linguistic strategies are used to present these views?

Text 6B

Ken Livingstone Mayoral campaign poster, 2012

Language, power and politics

Text 6C

Scotland in Union poster, 2015

Each of these texts shows how political parties can present their own stance through a process of delegitimation, whereby a positive self-image is constructed through the negative presentation of the opposition. According to linguists Paul Chilton and Christina Schäffner (1997), this is just one of the various functions of political discourse. They state that all political discourse is strategic and includes the use of:

- **Coercion:** if someone wields enough power, it can be used to control others. Forms of coercion are evident even if we are unaware of them through laws, regulations, or even commands. However, as Fairclough (2014) stated, it can be more effective to 'exercise power through the manufacture of consent … or at least acquiescence towards it'.

- **Resistance, opposition and protest:** the enforcement of power is not always passively received and less powerful groups can contest coercive power through a variety of linguistic strategies and physical action such as anti-government literature and protest rallies. Social media now allows us to exercise and communicate aspects of resistance more readily than has been possible before.

- **Legitimation and delegitimation:** within a democracy, those in power rule by consent; power is not enforced but agreed upon. Those who hold power must be seen to be legitimate and this is often achieved through positive self-presentation – politicians work hard to demonstrate that they have the necessary knowledge, expertise and ability to effectively represent their constituents. However, alongside legitimation, delegitimation is common, seeking to discredit others through attack of moral character, blame, or even exclusion, and this is a common feature of election campaigns.

Language and Power

- **Representation and misrepresentation:** Paul Chilton (2004) states that control of information is crucial when considering who holds political power. But to what extent is information presented fully and factually? Avoidance strategies or euphemisms are frequently employed so that audiences are provided with an element of truth and information. British Prime Minister Theresa May struggled to answer a question when she was being interviewed on a local UK radio station. Asked, 'Do you know what a mugwump is?', she responded 'What I recognise is that what we need in this country is strong and stable leadership'. Rather than admit to ignorance, May avoided the question completely, resorting to an almost prepared response linking back to her party's slogan for 'strong and stable leadership'.

> **KEY TERM**
>
> **Euphemisms:** words or phrases that are substituted for more direct words or phrases in an attempt to make things easier to accept or less embarrassing

6.1.2 CDA and persuasive language in political manifestos

Political posters, slogans and sound-bites are all ways that political ideas can be communicated in a digested form. But this can lead to misrepresentation and the electorate needs more information to get a full sense of what a political party stands for. Election manifestos are the platform that political parties use to present a full picture of their policies, as well as to explain what these policies aim to achieve. Persuasive techniques are often used in manifestos to present the party's aims and policies as part of an assumed shared ideology and thus in the public's best interests.

Look at Text 6D, an extract from the 2016 election manifesto of Plaid Cymru, which describes itself as the Party of Wales.

Text 6D

> 'Over the past five years we have been listening to what you want.
>
> Hundreds of thousands of you have told us about your concerns, your hopes, your frustrations and your dreams for your family, your community and for Wales.
>
> WE HAVE HEARD AND WE HAVE LISTENED.

Language, power and politics

This is how we will respond if you choose a Plaid Cymru Welsh Government in May

Thank you for talking to us. Thank you for making your opinions count.'

YOU TOLD US that it's simply not right that if you're suspected of having cancer you have to wait so long to be tested

SO WE WILL make sure that everyone in Wales is tested and given a diagnosis or the all clear within **28 days**

[…]

YOU TOLD US that you want to see our young people have the very best opportunities **to thrive and to work** here in Wales to boost our economy.

SO WE WILL fund our universities properly, cancel up to £18,000 of debt for those who work in Wales after graduating, and create 50,000 extra apprenticeships.

From Plaid Cymru Manifesto, 2016

Text 6D contains many persuasive linguistic strategies which are carefully shaped to suggest a shared ideology with the audience.

- The discourse is shaped as a 'conversation'.

- A semantic field associated with communication is used: 'we have been listening'; 'we have heard'; 'thank you for talking to us'; 'you told us'.

- A 'problem-solution' discourse structure is presented in adjacency pairs – 'you told us… so we will' – the audience has identified the problems and Plaid Cymru will solve them.

- Pronouns are used to establish a relationship with the audience: synthetic personalisation is used throughout with the use of 'you', but reference to 'hundreds and thousands of you' who have 'told us' suggests that this relationship is not synthetic at all, but a genuine one.

- Plaid Cymru is continually referred to collectively as 'we', establishing a unified front.

- The plural determiner 'our' aligns Plaid Cymru with the audience: 'our young people', 'our economy'.

- A semantic field of justice is used: 'it's simply not right', suggesting that this is the party that will address these injustices.

- Deontic modality is used throughout to suggest a determination to act: 'we will … make sure'; 'we will fund'.

Language and Power

> **KEY TERM**
>
> **Synthetic personalisation:** making it seem as if text receivers are being addressed as individuals rather than as a mass

> **PRACTICE QUESTION**
> **Persuasive techniques in political manifestos**
>
> Read Text 6E, which is taken from the opening section of the American Democratic Party platform. Identify examples of persuasive strategies used in this text. How are they used to present a shared ideology between the Democratic Party and the American public? Consider:
>
> - discourse structure
> - lexis and semantic choices
> - pronoun use
> - patterns of verb choices
> - listing
> - use of comparisons.

Text 6E

In 2016, Democrats meet in Philadelphia with the same basic belief that animated the Continental Congress when they gathered here 240 years ago: Out of many, we are one.

Under President Obama's leadership, and thanks to the hard work and determination of the American people, we have come a long way from the Great Recession and the Republican policies that triggered it. American businesses have now added 14.8 million jobs since private-sector job growth turned positive in early 2010. Twenty million people have gained health insurance coverage. The American auto industry just had its best year ever. And we are getting more of our energy from the sun and wind, and importing less oil from overseas.

But too many Americans have been left out and left behind. They are working longer hours with less security. Wages have barely budged and the racial wealth gap remains wide, while the cost of everything from childcare to a college education has continued to rise. And for too many families, the dream of home ownership is out of reach. As working people struggle, the top one percent accrues more wealth and more power.

Republicans in Congress have chosen gridlock and dysfunction over trying to find solutions to the real challenges we face. It's no wonder that so many feel like the system is rigged against them.

Democrats believe that cooperation is better than conflict, unity is better than division, empowerment is better than resentment, and bridges are better than walls.

It's a simple but powerful idea: we are stronger together.

Democrats believe we are stronger when we have an economy that works for everyone—an economy that grows incomes for working people, creates good-paying jobs, and puts a middle-class life within reach for more Americans. Democrats believe we can spur more sustainable economic growth, which will create good-paying jobs and raise wages. And we can have more economic fairness, so the rewards are shared broadly, not just with those at the top. We need an economy that prioritizes long-term investment over short-term profit-seeking, rewards the common interest over self-interest, and promotes innovation and entrepreneurship.

We believe that today's extreme level of income and wealth inequality—where the majority of the economic gains go to the top one percent and the richest 20 people in our country own more wealth than the bottom 150 million—makes our economy weaker, our communities poorer, and our politics poisonous.

And we know that our nation's long struggle with race is far from over. More than half a century after Rosa Parks sat and Dr. King marched and John Lewis bled, more than half a century after César Chávez, Dolores Huerta, and Larry Itliong organized, race still plays a significant role in determining who gets ahead in America and who gets left behind. We must face that reality and we must fix it.

Extract from American Democratic Party Platform, 2016

6.2 Political rhetoric in speeches, interviews and debates

There are many forms of public speaking and, in the field of politics, making speeches and engaging in debate are perhaps two of the most demanding, requiring sustained focus on a particular topic or issue in a way that will engage and inspire audiences. Whilst we would like to believe that political speeches are a means and opportunity for speakers to express their true beliefs and values, the more cynical might argue that politicians employ linguistic devices in an attempt to manipulate an audience into supporting the speaker's views.

6 Language and Power

6.2.1 Means of persuasion: ethos, pathos, logos

There has been a long standing interest in the power of rhetoric, and classical rhetoric was primarily developed as an 'art' to persuade people in a political assembly. The Greek philosopher Aristotle (384–322 BC) identified three means of persuasion that an effective orator must rely on:

- **ethos:** the personal character of the speaker

- **pathos:** arousing the emotions of the audience

- **logos:** patterns of reasoning provided by the words of the speech itself.

> **KEY TERM**
>
> **Rhetoric:** the art of persuasion or the means by which language is manipulated in order to persuade an audience

> **ACTIVITY 6.2**
>
> Analysing political speeches
>
> Former US President Obama's skill as an orator is widely acknowledged and has led to a renewed interest in the study of rhetoric. Text 6F is an extract from a speech in which he outlined his concerns about the lack of gun control measures in the United States.
>
> What strategies does Obama use to:
>
> - establish his own sense of character? (ethos)
>
> - arouse the emotions of the audience? (pathos)
>
> - provide a logically reasoned argument? (logos)

Text 6F

> The United States of America is not the only country on Earth with violent or dangerous people. We are not inherently more prone to violence. But we are the only advanced country on Earth that sees this kind of mass violence erupt with this kind of frequency. It doesn't happen in other advanced countries. It's not even close. And as I've said before, somehow we've become numb to it and we start thinking that this is normal.
>
> And instead of thinking about how to solve the problem, this has become one of our most polarized, partisan debates – despite the fact that there's

a general consensus in America about what needs to be done. That's part of the reason why, on Thursday, I'm going to hold a town hall meeting in Virginia on gun violence. Because my goal here is to bring good people on both sides of this issue together for an open discussion.

I'm not on the ballot again. I'm not looking to score some points. I think we can disagree without impugning other people's motives or without being disagreeable. We don't need to be talking past one another. But we do have to feel a sense of urgency about it. In Dr. King's words, we need to feel the 'fierce urgency of now.' Because people are dying. And the constant excuses for inaction no longer do, no longer suffice.

That's why we're here today. Not to debate the last mass shooting, but to do something to try to prevent the next one. To prove that the vast majority of Americans, even if our voices aren't always the loudest or most extreme, care enough about a little boy like Daniel to come together and take common-sense steps to save lives and protect more of our children.

Now, I want to be absolutely clear at the start – and I've said this over and over again, this also becomes routine, there is a ritual about this whole thing that I have to do – I believe in the Second Amendment. It's there written on the paper. It guarantees a right to bear arms. No matter how many times people try to twist my words around – I taught constitutional law, I know a little about this – I get it. But I also believe that we can find ways to reduce gun violence consistent with the Second Amendment.

I mean, think about it. We all believe in the First Amendment, the guarantee of free speech, but we accept that you can't yell 'fire' in a theater. We understand there are some constraints on our freedom in order to protect innocent people. We cherish our right to privacy, but we accept that you have to go through metal detectors before being allowed to board a plane. It's not because people like doing that, but we understand that's part of the price of living in a civilized society.

Extract from Barack Obama 'gun control' speech, 2016

6.2.2 Common features of rhetoric

Rhetorical features can be powerful when used within speeches, and it is worth exploring some of these in more detail.

Pronouns

Pronouns can be used in a variety of ways. They can be used to provide the speaker with a clear personal identity or can establish the speaker as part of a social group with the use of plural pronouns; for example, 'how do *we* begin to change these inequalities in *our* cultures?' (Michelle Obama, 2016). However, pronouns can also be used to reinforce the wide gulf between different social

6 Language and Power

groups. For instance, Frederick Douglass, when addressing the state of American slaves in the nineteenth century, stressed social and cultural differences through the use of pronouns to create a clear sense of separation between 'I', 'you' and 'us': 'I say it with a sad sense of disparity between us … Your high independence only reveals the immeasurable distance between us.'

Metaphors

Metaphors are a means by which we understand one concept in terms of another, and they are often used when exploring an abstract concept – they help us to understand something intangible using more familiar, concrete references. Metaphors are deliberately used in political discourse as they can allow for an abstract fear or threat to become a perceived reality. When former US president George W. Bush referred to a 'war on terror' he made the intangible 'terror' real by aligning it with war, something that we could physically fight. This is a powerful strategy, playing on the public's fears, and thus helping to encourage a collective action against this shared fear and very real 'terror'.

> **ACTIVITY 6.3**
> Metaphor in political speeches
> Identify the metaphors in Texts 6G–6I, extracts from different political speeches. Comment on the effects created by using these metaphors.

Text 6G

> Oh! Had I the ability, and could I reach the nation's ear, I would today pour out a fiery stream of biting ridicule, blasting reproach, withering sarcasm, and stern rebuke.
>
> Frederick Douglass

Text 6H

> The energy, the faith, the devotion which we bring to this endeavor will light our country and all who serve it – and the glow from that fire can truly light the world.
>
> From US President John F. Kennedy's inaugural address, 20 January 1961

Language, power and politics

Text 6I

> In the end, the American dream is not a sprint, or even a marathon, but a relay. Our families don't always cross the finish line in the span of one generation.
>
> From San Antonio Mayor Julian Castro's keynote address at the 2012 Democratic National Convention

Cohesion

Repeated words, ideas and themes are a useful cohesive strategy that can help to reinforce the message of a political speech, as in Text 6J.

Text 6J

> Never, never and never again shall it be that this beautiful land will again experience the oppression of one by another.
>
> From South African President Nelson Mandela's inaugural speech, 1994

Parallelism

The repetition of a repeated grammatical structure also creates shape and cohesion, as used in Text 6K. The underlined words illustrate the main focus of Kennedy's speech, that not only allies but also adversaries must work together to ensure global peace. This is reinforced with a repeated semantic field based on togetherness and unity.

Text 6K

> <u>Let both sides</u> explore what problems unite us instead of belaboring those problems which divide us. <u>Let both sides</u>, for the first time, formulate serious and precise proposals for the inspection and control of arms--and bring the absolute power to destroy other nations under the absolute control of all nations. <u>Let both sides</u> seek to invoke the wonders of science instead of its terrors. Together let us explore the stars, conquer the deserts, eradicate disease, tap the ocean depths and encourage the arts and commerce. <u>Let both sides</u> unite to heed in all corners of the earth the command of Isaiah-- to 'undo the heavy burdens . . . (and) let the oppressed go free.'
>
> From John F. Kennedy's inaugural address, 20 January 1961

6 Language and Power

Three-part lists

These present information in three stages. A key idea or argument is introduced at stage 1; stage 2 emphasises the importance and relevance of this point; and stage 3 reinforces the first two points, while also signalling that the argument has been concluded. Three-part structures provide a resonance for the audience, making them more memorable, as seen in these examples:

- 'Friends, Romans, Countrymen', Julius Caesar
- 'Blood, sweat and tears', Winston Churchill
- 'Stay strong, work hard, and keep pushing forward', Michelle Obama.

> **RESEARCH QUESTION**
> Rhetoric
>
> Many political speeches are famous for their skilful use of rhetoric. Find a good example – many are available online in their spoken form and some will have an accompanying transcript. You may wish to focus on a key political figure from the past or present, such as Winston Churchill or Nelson Mandela, or you may wish to focus on speeches delivered to the United Nations by famous people, such as Emma Watson's speech on gender equality or Malala Yousafzai's speech calling on education for all.
>
> What linguistic features does the speaker use to influence and persuade the audience?
>
> You may wish to extend your study of political speeches further by examining different speeches from different times. For example, different inaugural speeches may reflect different social concerns based on the era they were delivered. Or, topics such as gender roles, education, domestic or foreign affairs may reflect changing social attitudes.

6.2.3 The political interview

Politicians do not just speak in isolation with no danger of interruption, and a key type of political discourse is the political interview. Media interviews, in which a television or radio interviewer will put the seasoned politician under the spotlight, make use of a very specific political discourse.

The media interview fulfils a vital purpose and function. In this situation the interviewer has the power to set the agenda, lead the discussion and address the questions and issues that they feel the audience has a right to know. The roles

Language, power and politics

that the interviewer and interviewee play create an almost theatrical performance: the politician is often made to appear as the villain of the piece, fighting for survival against the righteous attack of the interviewer, who is determined to arrive at the 'truth' behind political decisions and policies. The interviewer must probe and interrogate the politician using a variety of questioning techniques whilst the politician will strive to present a positive image of themselves and their political party. The interviewer aims to address the public's political concerns, or issues raised in the media. They must also be aware of the medium: if the interview is to be aired on television or radio, then it must be entertaining. Thus, some linguistic choices designed to provoke and antagonise will have been deliberately structured to produce a verbal sparring match – there would be little entertainment if the interview was a smooth running cooperative discourse.

Question techniques

The formation of questions is not a straightforward matter. Simple use of an interrogative will not always elicit a straightforward, direct response, particularly in the political arena where those in power exercise power over knowledge. A number of different question techniques are frequently used in political interviews, as shown in Tables 6.1 and 6.2.

Table 6.1: Direct questioning techniques

Question type	Purpose	Example
Open questions	Can elicit any response	*How will you be able to improve employment opportunities for those who are under 25 years old?*
Polar questions	Will elicit either a *yes* or *no* response	*Are you going to help those who genuinely need help?*
Optional questions	Will elicit a response based around a limited number of options	*Will you follow the old rules? Or will you vote for a new way?*

Table 6.2: Indirect questioning techniques

Question type	Purpose	Example
Declarative with rising intonation	The declarative allows for an assertion of 'facts'; the rising intonation questions the validity of those 'facts'	*You state that, under your government, crime statistics have fallen?*

6 Language and Power

Question type	Purpose	Example
Declarative with tag question	The tag question narrows the range of responses that may be allowable	*You told us that the economy would improve, didn't you? But it hasn't, has it?*

Polar and optional questions tend to be favoured during political interviews as these can direct and control the agenda and structure of the interview. Open questions can lead to digression, with a politician perhaps opting to steer the topic to an agenda more suited to their own purposes.

Whilst the interviewer uses questions to control an interview, this does not mean that the interviewee remains powerless. A number of different strategies may be employed to avoid responding directly:

- A question may be completely ignored.
- The legitimacy of a question can be questioned.
- A prepared response may be offered which does not address the question that was actually asked.
- A response to a question can become completely mired in an overly lengthy statement, thus making the actual answer to the question unclear.

Face, politeness and cooperation

Political discourse can also be explored using some of the concepts you looked at in Chapter 2: Erving Goffman's face theory (1967), and Penelope Brown and Stephen Levinson's politeness principle (1987).

Face theory is a particularly useful way of examining political discourse. Positive face is the desire to be approved of, and this is certainly relevant for politicians, who need to demonstrate that they are deserving of their electorate's support. Not only does the politician need to present their own positive face, but also ensure that they present the positive face of the political party they represent. Of course, face-threatening behaviour may occur, where approval may not be shown and direct challenge of positive face is a common interview strategy. For example: 'When it comes to making the big decisions, do you have what it takes to act in the best interests of the people? You won't be able to dodge that. You have to stay firm. Can you do that?' Here, face threat is presented through the implication that the interviewee does not have what it takes to make 'the big decisions'.

Brown and Levinson's politeness theory (1987) proposed that speakers will make use of strategies to avoid or mitigate face-threatening acts by using positive politeness or negative politeness strategies. Positive politeness strategies seek to minimise the threat to positive face by seeking to claim common ground and making the hearer feel a sense of closeness. Some strategies of positive politeness include statements of solidarity and friendship, compliments and avoidance of disagreement. Negative politeness strategies seek to minimise imposition on the hearer by using hedging, or being indirect, pessimistic or apologetic. It can certainly be interesting to see how an interviewer will align themselves with a politician during a political interview: will they strike a cooperative frame which recognises and values the roles of each participant? Or are politeness strategies avoided, so that positive face is threatened?

Paul Grice's conversational maxims (1975) suggest that speakers cooperate to achieve mutual conversational ends by following four conversational maxims:

- **Maxim of quantity:** give the most helpful amount of information
- **Maxim of quality:** do not say what you believe to be false
- **Maxim of relation:** make contributions relevant
- **Maxim of manner:** communicate in a clear and orderly way

Conversational maxims are frequently violated or flouted. If we violate a maxim we do so surreptitiously so that other people don't know. If we flout a maxim, we do so overtly so that it is obvious that the maxim has been broken. Flouting a maxim is often done through implicature – the hearer is expected to infer some extra meaning from what is actually stated.

KEY TERM
Implicature: an implied meaning that has to be inferred by a speaker as a result of one of the maxims being broken

ACTIVITY 6.4
Analysing a political interview

Text 6L is taken from a televised interview between the interviewer Krishnan Guru-Murthy (KG-M) from the UK's Channel 4 news and David Davis (DD), Secretary of State for Exiting the European Union (EU). They are discussing Britain's departure from the EU.

What questioning techniques does KG-M use to control the agenda of the interview? What strategies does DD use to present a positive face image? Are any face-threatening strategies used? Do KG-M and DD abide by politeness and cooperative maxims?

6 Language and Power

Text 6L

KG-M:	were you at work on Monday (.) or were you out campaigning
DD:	Monday (.) I was out campaigning (.) I was in Erdington I think initially (.) er then I did er some broadcasts then I came back
KG-M:	because on Monday the EU issued its two big documents on the negotiation (.) position (.) and you'd have thought that you as the Brexit secretary (.) were sitting down to have a look at them and read them
DD:	it's the wonders of modern technology er (.) Mr Guru-Murthy (.) that you can actually er read things on ipads on the train
KG-M:	but the point is
DD:	I don't need to read them in the studio like Mr Corbyn (.) I do read them on the train (.) and that's what I did that day
KG-M:	this election
DD:	I know the point you're trying to make but you're failing to make
KG-M:	has been a huge distraction (.) hasn't it
DD:	sorry
KG-M:	this election has been a huge distraction (.) to your job (.) not preparing for the Brexit (.) for the negotiations beginning eleven days after the election
DD:	one of the points one of the points (.) would you like the answer (.) one of the points to this election (.) is to reinforce Theresa May's hand (.) so eleven days after this election is over (.) when she goes if she's elected Prime Minister and you've made some points about about surveys today (.) but if she's elected and she's our representative (.) she'll be there fully prepared (.) with ten months of preparation behind her (.) and she'll have a mandate (.) and that's a very important point (.) a mandate to carry out the negotiation in the way she has described (.) a free trade area (.) customs agreement (.) a continuing agreement on security (.) all the things we've laid out in two white papers (.) er in a major letter to the commission (.) that's what we're doing (.) that's why she's the person to lead this country
KG-M:	in March you admitted that you hadn't costed the economic impact (1) of no deal (.) even though you keep saying no deal is better than a bad deal (.) have you done one yet
DD:	what you're (.) you're summarising something let me tell you what it is (1) if you're going to do a costing of something like

this you've got to cost everything (.) you've got to cost what the changes in exports are (.) both to the EU (.) and to the world at large (.) it's very plain that after we leave the EU we'll be able to enhance our ability to export to the rest of the world (.) that will be a benefit (.) what we're aiming to do is to maintain the most frictionless free trade to Europe with no tariffs and minimal customs restrictions (.) **that** should preserve our market there (.) so I can't see where there should be a cost to it (.) but that's a point (.) you've got to work those things out first (.) forecasts without doing that first are just guesswork (.) and I don't do guesswork

KG-M: okay (.) so we haven't got one yet

Krishnan Guru-Murthy interviews David Davis, Secretary of State for Exiting the EU, *Channel 4 News*, 31 May 2017

6.2.4 Parliamentary debate

Political discourse functions in a particularly distinctive way during parliamentary or congressional proceedings. On the surface, the interaction between participants can appear to be controlled, cooperative discourse. However, closer examination reveals exchanges which are rooted in tradition and ritual, with clearly defined 'rules' for agenda setting, turn-taking and interaction, where even direct address and challenging statements need to be carefully couched so as not to break with convention.

Take a look at Text 6M, an extract from a parliamentary debate in the UK House of Commons. The Under-Secretary for State for Welfare Delivery, Caroline Nokes, was asked to address Government plans to remove automatic entitlement to housing benefit for 18–21-year-olds. (C stands for the Conservative Party; L for the Labour Party.)

Text 6M

Justin Tomlinson (C):	What are the Government doing to ensure that this policy supports young people who are in work?
Caroline Nokes (C):	My honourable friend is right to mention young people who are in work. Anybody who is working 16 hours a week or more at the national minimum wage equivalent will be exempt.
Edward Miliband (L):	I think we should call this what it is: a nasty, vindictive policy that will make injustice worse, from a Government who said that they would tackle burning injustice. Will the Minister now

6 Language and Power

	answer the question that my right honourable friend the Member for Wentworth and Dearne (John Healey) asked? No impact assessment has been published for the measure—inexplicably, in my view. Will she tell the House what advice she has received from her officials about the impact on homelessness of this proposal?
Caroline Nokes (C):	The Department has, of course, met all its requirements under the public sector equality duty. Equality assessment information has been received and shared with the Social Security Advisory Committee, which chose not to consult on this.
Desmond Swayne (C):	Young people in their first jobs cannot afford their own accommodation, so they share with other young people or they stay at home. Why should it be different for people who are out of work?
Caroline Nokes (C):	My right honourable friend makes exactly the point that underpins this policy. We want young people in work and young people out of work to be making the same choices about where they are going to live.
Luciana Berger (L):	I think that anyone listening to this urgent question would, frankly, be appalled by the responses that we have had thus far from the Minister. She has not answered any of the questions that were rightly asked by my right honourable friend the Member for Wentworth and Dearne (John Healey). Will she tell us why the equality impact assessment has not been published and when she will bring it forward, so that we can all see exactly the rationale behind this ridiculous policy?
Caroline Nokes (C):	I think I have answered that. The Department has engaged extensively at ministerial and official level with stakeholders. We announced this measure in the summer Budget. There is no duty on us to share the impact assessment with the House, but we did share it with the Social Security Advisory Committee.
Lucy Allan (C):	Will the Minister confirm that care leavers will not be affected by these changes?

Language, power and politics

Caroline Nokes (C):	My honourable friend makes a really important point about care leavers. Absolutely, they are exempt from this policy.
Clive Betts (L):	One of the exemptions in the regulations where housing benefit can still be paid is if 'in the opinion of the Secretary of State it is inappropriate for the renter to live with each of their parents'. Does the Secretary of State assume that this exemption will automatically apply where the parents refuse to have their child living with them?
Caroline Nokes (C):	Absolutely. That is a point. A very important exemption is included, so where that is inappropriate—where a parent cannot or will not accommodate their child—such people will be exempt from the policy.

You will have noticed from the text the extremely ordered nature of the exchange.

- Turn-taking progresses in a very structured way, with each speaker allowed a turn. Development or rebuttal only takes place once the speaker has concluded their remarks.

- Forms of address are carefully applied. The opening question here does not directly address the Under-Secretary; instead, it is directed at 'the government'. When the speaker makes a statement, she prefaces her statement with 'The Department', thus acting as the spokesperson of the whole department or government rather than as an individual.

- Second-person pronoun *you* is avoided, as are personal address terms. Instead, speakers are addressed according to their role: 'My honourable friend'; 'the Minister'. This establishes an air of extreme formality, which is maintained even if the speaker's comments are challenged.

- Questions are carefully shaped, according to the political party representative who poses the question. For instance, compare:

    1 'Will the Minister confirm that care leavers will not be affected by these changes?'

    2 'Will she tell us why the equality impact assessment has not been published and when she will bring it forward, so that we can all see exactly the rationale behind this ridiculous policy?'

The first question simply asks the speaker to 'confirm' which opens the floor for development of an issue that is perhaps already understood by those involved in this exchange. The second question is more challenging, asking

Language and Power

the minister to 'explain' and justify key aspects of the policy in more detail. It is perhaps evident which of these two questions is presented by someone from the same political party and which is from the opposition.

- The questions asked by Edward Miliband are particularly interesting: he prefaces his questions with a personal response to the government policy under discussion, thus making his position about the issue clear. He then goes on to ask not one, but two questions. He actually responds to his own opening question: 'Will the Minister now answer the question…?' with his assessment of the issue: 'No impact assessment has been published for the measure'. This is a common discourse strategy – to ask a question which is then immediately answered in a negative or affirmative manner depending on which stance the speaker holds. This denies the main speaker, here Caroline Nokes, the opportunity to respond and defend her position. His subsequent question: 'Will she tell the House what advice she has received from her officials…?' refocuses the main point of the debate, and reminds all those present that Caroline Nokes is merely a spokesperson for her party, not the person actually making decisions herself. This seeks to undermine her position and role here.

- Caroline Nokes uses a largely positive semantic field when addressing questions from those within the Conservative party: 'My right honourable friend makes exactly the point that underpins this policy'; 'absolutely'; 'My honourable friend is right to mention', showing a level of consensus and solidarity between party members.

- Her responses to questions from other political parties are perhaps less positive. Her response to Luciana Berger: 'I think I have answered that' serves as a reprimand, suggesting that not enough attention has been paid to her earlier comments. Her response to Edward Miliband: 'The Department has, of course, met all its requirements' adopts a distanced approach, deflecting attention away from herself and onto the department as a whole instead.

- The language used by Caroline Nokes' party colleagues is fairly supportive, with questions which seek to further the discussion of the topic. This contrasts with the language of those in opposing political parties: 'I think that anyone listening to this urgent question would, frankly, be appalled by the responses we have had thus far from the Minister'; 'I think we should call this what it is: a nasty, vindictive policy that will make injustice worse'. These contributions make use of highly emotive language, laden with negative connotations, reflecting not only their own responses to the issue at hand, but also assuming a wider negative response: 'anyone listening… would be appalled'. It is notable that Nokes herself is not criticised or overtly targeted, merely the policies that she is presenting and supporting.

This is a short example of how parliamentary debates are organised and reveals the intricacies of language use in an environment where what one says and how one says it is carefully monitored and controlled, with only very particular contributions being allowable within the context. For instance, first names are not permitted, no matter how close the relationship between the speakers. These parliamentary debates may appear to be a rather intricate and laborious way of discussing political issues and policies, but this system does allow all to air their views without fear of interruption. Even challenges are couched in a formulaic, almost ritualistic way, allowing conflict to be resolved within a professional arena without fear of reprisal.

RESEARCH QUESTION
Political discourse

You have examined many forms of political discourse, focusing on how established political figures and parties use language in different contexts. However, everyone is involved with politics in most aspects of everyday life, and political protestors, pressure groups or demonstrators all make use of similar linguistic strategies to those examined above.

Examine some of the political literature that is available in your local area. This may be campaign material to save local resources such as libraries, speeches presented at local council meetings about changes to the local environment, or adverts of local party political broadcasts.

Focusing closely on your chosen political text, consider how political discourse is structured and framed to influence and persuade the local audience.

Wider reading

You can read more about power and political language in the following books:

Beard, A. (2000) *The Language of Politics*. Oxon: Routledge.

Charteris-Black, J. (2014) *Analysing Political Speeches: Rhetoric, Discourse and Metaphor*. London: Palgrave Macmillan.

Chilton, P. (2004) *Analysing Political Discourse: Theory and Practice*. London: Routledge.

Simpson, P. and Mayr, A. (2010) *Language and Power: A Resource Book for Students*. Abingdon, Routledge.

Thomas, L. and Wareing, S. (2012) *Language, Society and Power: An Introduction*. London, Routledge.

Wodak, R. and Meyer, M. (2016) *Methods of Critical Discourse Studies* (Third edition). London: Sage.

Chapter 7
Language, power and the law

In this chapter you will:

- Consider some of the functions and purposes of legal discourse
- Examine some of the linguistic features associated with legal situations
- Explore some of the ways that legal language is used to enforce power and control

Language, power and the law

It seems obvious to state that the law is a powerful entity – it is an established institution, rooted in tradition and authorised by governing bodies. Its complex linguistic structures render it opaque and shrouded in mystery that only the very few are party to. And yet we are all subject to the law and, in order to comply with legal principles, we need to be aware of what these legal processes are and how they apply to us. The law is something that every citizen of the world must have a basic understanding of in order to function within local society and as a member of a global community, and yet we often do so with only partial awareness and understanding of the intricacies of legal discourse.

There have been many attempts to simplify official language. In the UK, the Plain English Campaign has worked hard to make many aspects of communication accessible to the masses. The Plain Writing Act of 2010, implemented in the United States, states that 'Government documents issued to the public must be written clearly', thereby ensuring that all citizens can gain access to Government information and services. Despite these initiatives, legal language remains impenetrable to the majority, creating a power asymmetry that can seem insurmountable.

In this chapter, you will consider some of the linguistic devices that make the language of the law so dense, and consider some of the ways that legal language is used in written and spoken legal contexts.

> **KEY TERM**
>
> **Power asymmetry:** a power imbalance between speakers shown by the unequal way they address each other

7.1 A register rooted in tradition

One of the aspects of legal language that appears so confusing to the lay person is the proliferation of seemingly obscure terms such as *habeas corpus*, *decree nisi* or *subpoena,* alongside an evident archaic register characterised by terms such as *heretofore, herein, to wit, aforesaid*, which are commonplace in court proceedings and legal documents. Legal language contains many such terms as a highly specialised register, many of which are not found in any other form of modern discourse. Thus, legal discourse remains extremely specialised and exclusive, employed only by those who are part of an in-group. This creates a level of professional cohesion, but can also be extremely alienating for those who are not members of this very powerful group.

It has always been necessary to establish laws to ensure the smooth running of any society. And with such a long standing legal tradition, administrations

Language and Power

and law courts worldwide draw on many features embedded into their own unique histories. This is certainly the case with the UK legal system. The English language, often described as a mongrel language, has its origins in Anglo-Saxon, French and Latin, and has borrowed extensively from all of these languages. While many borrowed terms have been naturalised so that we no longer consider them 'foreign' loans, legal language has retained many borrowed terms in their original form. This goes some way to explain the proliferation of Latin terms such as *habeas corpus* in legal discourse. Long regarded as an authoritative, learned language, Latin confers a gravitas and legitimacy to official documents and proceedings which perhaps would be absent if only Anglo-Saxon forms were used. French loanwords, such as *bailiff, counsel, justice, verdict* are also prevalent in legal discourse, a legacy of the ruling French classes following the Norman Conquest of 1066. French was used in courts of law during this time; it was considered to be the language of justice and seen as more precise and expressive than Anglo-Saxon. It was only in 1362 that the Statute of Pleading called for English law to be: 'pleaded, shewed, defended, answered, debated and judged in the English Tongue'. Ironically, the Statute itself was composed in French!

The development of the English language has seen an easy intermingling of Anglo-Saxon, French and Latin forms, and the language of the law reflects this rich and diverse history. A notable feature of legal discourse is the use of binomials, or pairings of words using the conjunction *and*, such as 'fit and proper', and 'goods and chattels'. Both these examples contain Anglo-Saxon terms (*fit, goods*) alongside French borrowed terms (*proper, chattels*). This mix of terms reflects the varied language of users in earlier times, so that no one was exempt from understanding the law. Rhymed or paired phrases such as 'to have and to hold', typical of Anglo-Saxon kennings, are also a key feature of modern legal language.

KEY TERMS

Archaic: an older word or style of language no longer in everyday use

Register: a variety of language that is associated with a particular situation of use

In-group: an exclusive group of people with shared interests or identity

Binomial: two-part pairs or phrases, with words linked by the conjunction *and*

Kenning: a two-word compound expression, often providing a metaphorical meaning to an object or entity

So, whilst at first glance legal language appears to be a confusion of styles and registers, a closer look at the origins of the language can help you understand some of the different languages that have helped to form modern legal language.

7.2 Functions and features of legal language in written discourse

Legal language is sometimes referred to as legalese, a term that suggests the dense and impenetrable nature of the discourse, which might sometimes appear as though it is designed to deliberately baffle the lay person, who has no specialised knowledge.

> **KEY TERM**
>
> **Legalese:** the formal, technical language of legal documents, sometimes considered deliberately alienating for those not working within the legal profession

But it can be argued that this level of complexity is essential to prevent confusion or ambiguity. Holders of a legal document must be certain that it is explicit and precise, otherwise the legitimacy and reliability of that document could be called into question. A legal document or contract must be watertight and cover all eventualities so that there can be no direct challenge. Thus, language that might seem obscure and incomprehensible is not just allowable given the context, but may well be necessary to avoid equivocation or vagueness which may allow the document to be contested. Linguist David Crystal (2010) states that '[legal] statements have to be so phrased that we can see their general applicability, yet be specific enough to apply to individual circumstances ... Above all they have to be expressed in such a way that people can be certain of the intention of the law respecting their rights and duties.'

Text 7A, which is an extract from the beginning of a will, contains many features which are typical of written legal language.

Text 7A

> THE LAST WILL AND TESTAMENT OF JOSEPH ALEXANDER DAVIES
>
> I give everything I own at my death to my trustees upon the following trusts
>
> (a) to pay my debts funeral and testamentary expenses and any tax due as a result of my death
>
> (b) divide my residuary estate between such of my children as are living at my death and if more than one in equal shares
>
> (c) in the event of any of my children dying before me leaving a child or children alive at my death then such children shall take in equal shares the share that his / her or their parent would have taken if he or she had survived me

7 Language and Power

This rather convoluted text might seem baffling and you might think that the following would be clearer:

> 'Once all outstanding costs have been made, all remaining assets should be given equally to my children. If any of them die before me, then my grandchildren will receive that share.'

Whilst the second version is certainly easier to read, there is great potential here for misinterpretation. Which costs are covered by the will? Which share would the grandchildren receive? And which grandchildren are intended here? The children of the dead child? Or any other grandchildren? So, whilst the original text may seem cumbersome and awkward, the language is explicit and unambiguous and ensures that Joseph Alexander Davies' final wishes are indeed met.

There are many different types of legal text, all fulfilling very specific purposes. Three broad types can be identified:

- legislative documents, having the power to make laws and regulations, such as the Freedom of Information Act, 2000
- private law documents, including all personal or business contracts
- procedural documents, or the rules which a court must follow.

> **ACTIVITY 7.1**
> **Types of written legal document**
> Look at the following list of legal texts and decide which of the broad categories listed above each falls into:
>
> - Last will and testament
> - Music copyright licence
> - Rental tenancy agreement
> - The Press Commission Code of Conduct
> - Document providing details to a jury about codes of behaviour during a trial
> - Consumer Protection Act.

We encounter legal texts all the time, and we are so exposed to them that we often do not recognise the significance of them. Any time we purchase a new mobile phone contract or renew a television licence, legal language is paramount

Language, power and the law

to ensure that power roles are not abused: consumers' rights need to be protected but, should the consumer default on an agreement, then consequences are in place to make sure that organisations are also protected. Thus, although at first glance, power within the discourse may suggest that power roles are asymmetrical, in fact both parties hold a degree of power which is carefully balanced. And this means that a particular style has developed that seems particularly dense, with lengthy sentences containing multiple clauses, extensive listing and repetition to make certain that all eventualities are addressed, elaborate noun phrases to ensure clarity, and use of conjunctions in place of punctuation markers.

Take a look at Text 7B, which is taken from the terms and conditions of a credit card agreement, as set out by a British bank. It illustrates many of the features typical of legal contracts.

Text 7B

B9. Ending this agreement

We may end this agreement immediately if:

- there is illegal or fraudulent activity on or connected to the account;
- you are or may be behaving improperly – for example, in a threatening or abusive way;
- you have seriously or repeatedly broken this agreement in any other way.

In any other case, we will give you two months' notice in writing. You can give us notice to end the agreement at any time. If either of us gives notice to end this agreement:

- you must stop making any transactions, destroy all cards, cancel any recurring transaction instructions and repay your full balance;
- the agreement will continue until you have repaid all amounts you owe us including amounts added to your account after notice was given; and
- if your standard interest rates are linked to the Bank of England Base Rate, they will no longer be linked to it from the last working day of the month in which your notice was given. But if you give us notice in the last 7 working days of the month, we may not be able to prevent any Base Rate changes in that month taking effect on your account.

Extract from Halifax Credit Card terms and conditions

7 Language and Power

Pronouns are used carefully throughout this text, and this is a common way of presenting power behind and within a text. This text addresses the audience directly, throughout. This places responsibility on the audience, suggesting that they are accountable for their own actions. This is reinforced through the use of directives aimed at the audience, such as:

- '<u>you have seriously or repeatedly broken</u> this agreement'
- '<u>you must stop making</u> any transactions'
- 'until <u>you have repaid</u> all amounts you owe us'.

The bank itself is not named, but the collective pronouns 'we' and 'us' are used throughout. This effectively creates an 'us' versus 'you' situation – 'we' (the bank) provide the service which 'you' (the customer) are obliged to follow in the ways set out in this agreement. The collective but almost anonymous 'we' creates a degree of objectivity that is a characteristic of legal texts and contracts.

Modal auxiliary verbs and conditional clauses also feature heavily in legal discourse, stressing elements which are or are not allowable given the terms of an agreement:

- 'we <u>may</u> end this agreement immediately <u>if</u> there is illegal or fraudulent activity…'
- 'you <u>must</u> stop making any transactions'
- '<u>If</u> either of us gives notice to end…'
- '<u>If</u> your standard interest rates are linked to the Bank of England Base Rate…'
- '<u>If</u> you give us notice in the last 7 working days…'.

Modal auxiliary verbs clearly state the role of both the bank and the customer, and the conditional clauses aim to set out a number of alternatives and possible scenarios. This means that the bank is essentially 'protected' from any unforeseen situation and it is able to safeguard its own interests.

These language features are typically found in most 'private law' documents and illustrate power within the discourse. There are other notable features of 'legalese' which help to present a tone of top-down authority, evident even in the graphology and typography of a text (as shown in Text 7C). A lack of visual imagery can seem a little austere to the lay person, but puts increased emphasis on the use of upper case or bold typography, so that the most important aspects of a legal text are immediately seen.

Text 7C

PROPERTY FIRST, High Street, Watford UK

AST Agreement – 178 Main Street, Watford UK

DATE of Agreement – 19th July 2018

ASSURED SHORTHOLD TENANCY AGREEMENT

For letting a ~ furnished flat on an Assured Shorthold Tenancy under Part 1 of the Housing Act 1988 as amended by the Housing Act 1996.

This agreement is made the _____ day of _____

1. Particulars

    1.1. Parties

        1.1.1. The Landlord

        MR J SMITH

        Address: _____

        _____

        The "Landlord" shall include the Landlord's successors in title and assigns.

        1.1.2. The Tenant

        MRS MARYLAND

        Address: _____

        _____

        1.1.3. The Guarantor

        Not Any.

        1.1.4. The Landlord's Agent

        The "Landlord's Agent" shall mean PROPERTY FIRST or such other agents as the Landlord may from time to time appoint.

        Where the party consists of more than one person the obligations apply to and are enforceable against them jointly and severally.

    1.2. The Landlord lets and the Tenant takes the Property for the Term at the Rent payable upon the terms and conditions of this agreement.

7 Language and Power

Legal documents contain a high number of nouns and noun phrases to reflect the need for clarity. Typically anaphora is used in other texts to avoid repetition and offer varied expression. In legal texts, where transparency and precision is key, anaphora is rarely found as substituting one word for another could lead to ambiguity. Frequent use of nouns and explicit naming of participants often results in extensive repetition, and even listing to ensure that all eventualities are taken into account.

> **KEY TERM**
>
> **Anaphora:** the use of a word referring back to a word used earlier in a text to avoid repetition

As with any profession, a special register uses technical terms limited to the field of law, including fixed expressions such as 'beyond reasonable doubt'. Some terms gain a specific meaning when used in a legal context which is not reflected in non-legal usage. For instance, 'suit' simply refers to an outfit of clothing, but in a legal context it refers to legal action. To 'strike' something is to delete it from the record, not to physically attack something.

These kinds of language features help to create a legal style that should be regarded as functional rather than decorative or deliberately rhetorical.

> **ACTIVITY 7.2**
>
> **Analysing legal documents**
>
> Study Texts 7D–7G, taken from various terms and agreements that we are frequently exposed to. What language features are used to enforce rules and codes of behaviour?
>
> Are any language features used which might suggest that the audience's rights are also being protected?

Text 7D

> We will share personal information with companies, organisations or individuals if we have a belief in the good faith that access, use, preservation or disclosure of the information is reasonably necessary to meet any applicable law, regulation, legal process or enforceable government request.
>
> Extract from Google terms and conditions

Language, power and the law

Text 7E

We believe in the power of communications to make a better world. That means we want our services to help customers freely express themselves and share information. But that shouldn't be at the expense of other people's safety and rights.

That's why we have a few rules on how our services can and can't be used. This policy explains them, what we might do if you break them, and what to do if you've got any concerns.

Extract from British Telecommunications plc Consumer Acceptable Use Policy

Text 7F

The Library reserves the right to take appropriate action to ensure compliance with the policy, including withdrawing the right to access the Internet. We will contact the police in cases which involve illegal activity.

Extract from Hounslow Library Code of Conduct

Text 7G

If the service on which you have booked to travel is cancelled or severely disrupted you may be entitled to compensation or a refund. If the train company allows us to issue this refund on their behalf, we shall do so. If not, we will provide you with the contact details of the relevant train company and you will need to make a claim directly with the train company concerned.

Extract from Virgin Trains terms and conditions

7.3 Spoken language in the courtroom

American law professor Peter Tiersma (1999) stated that: 'lawyers are, on the one hand, among the most eloquent users of the English language, while, on the other, they are perhaps its most notorious abusers. Why is it that lawyers, who may excel in communicating with a jury, seem incapable of writing an ordinary, comprehensible English sentence in a contract, deed, or will?'

You have seen that legal language certainly can seem to be overly complex with impenetrable structures and phrasing, and yet language within a courtroom setting serves a very different function. Lawyers must choose language to persuade jury members to accept their arguments and use probing questions to interrogate witnesses and elicit the facts about a case, all while trying to engage with a number

7 Language and Power

of different audiences. A trial lawyer will be communicating with a judge, fellow lawyers, the jury, the defendant and a variety of witnesses, often including those offering expert testimony. At the same time they must also be aware of the wider audience, including the families of those involved in the case, and even those who just have an interest in the case or in legal proceedings. Alan Durant and Janny Leung (2016: 71) describe trials as 'a battle, contest, performance, or process of storytelling'. It is the very nature of legal language within the courtroom as all of these things that make it such a fascinating area of linguistic study.

The legal system of countries such as the UK, the United States of America, Australia, India and many other countries that have seen British colonial influence is one based on adversarial law. In an adversarial court of law, an impartial judge or jury will attempt to determine the truth about a case on the basis of the arguments presented by two legal counsels, and pass judgement accordingly. Thus, roles are clearly defined, and all those involved will use specific language techniques to achieve their purposes.

7.3.1 Opening and closing statements

Opening and closing statements form a pivotal role in courtroom proceedings. It is often said that a 'good story must have a strong opening' and trials subscribe to this maxim. Opening statements allow both defending and prosecuting lawyers to summarise the main aspects of the case that will be explored more fully during the trial. This often takes the form of a narrative – a story that the audience, or jury, can engage with, allowing them to almost imagine themselves as part of the events that took place. The narrative will also lead to a projection of the likely outcome of a 'guilty' or 'not guilty' verdict. This is an opportunity to influence the jury about the legitimacy of the case, about the character of the defendant, and even about the credibility of the lawyers themselves. Thus, although narrative in approach, there will be strong persuasive elements, designed to get the jury on side and to ultimately win the case.

ACTIVITY 7.3

Analysing opening statements

American energy company Enron was the subject of a financial scandal and, in 2006, former CEOs Kenneth Lay and Jeffrey Skilling were prosecuted by the US government for fraud and insider trading.

Read Text 7H, the prosecution's opening statement at the trial. How does the speaker attempt to convince the audience of Kenneth Lay and Jeffrey Skilling's guilt? How does the speaker present the victims of their alleged fraud?

Language, power and the law

In particular, focus on the use of:

- emotive language
- modal verbs
- repetition
- modifiers
- varied sentence types.

Text 7H

> The government will take you inside the doors of what was once the seventh largest corporation in this country, Enron. In the year before Enron declared bankruptcy, two men at the helm of the company told lie after lie about the true financial condition of Enron, lies that propped up the value of their own stock holdings and lies that deprived the common investors of information that they needed to make fully informed decisions about their own Enron stock. You will see that the Defendants Lay and Skilling knew key facts about the true condition of Enron, facts that the investing public did not know. With that information, Defendants Lay and Skilling sold tens of millions of dollars of their own Enron stock. The victims in this case, the investing public, their employees, those who did not have that information, those who were not able to sell their stock before Enron entered bankruptcy were not as fortunate as these two men. These men are Defendants Ken Lay and Jeffrey Skilling. This is a simple case. It is not about accounting. It is about lies and choices. This case will show you that these Defendants worked to lie and to mislead. They violated the duty of trust placed in them. They violated it by telling lie after lie about the true financial condition of Enron.

Closing statements are similarly powerful. After what can often be quite lengthy courtroom proceedings, a closing statement seeks to summarise the most crucial elements of a case. It is also an opportunity to rebut the opponent's arguments, explain how the evidence that has been presented meets all legal requirements for the final verdict, and direct the jury into making a decision based on the testimonies that have been presented. Crucially, it is the last opportunity a lawyer has to influence the judge and jury, and so must be carefully constructed.

7.3.2 Questioning and presupposition

One of the key features of courtroom discourse is the way that language choices are shaped to elicit 'truth'. This may be through careful use of questioning techniques, through presupposition, or even reformulation of witness statements.

Language and Power

In a conventional adjacency pair pattern, questions are designed to elicit an answer to the question, and the respondent provides that response, allowing both parties to take up fairly equal floor space. In courtroom discourse, the function of questions is more complex than this, with the formulation of questions that are designed to provoke, to contest, to lead and to coerce the witness. Open-ended questions, such as those beginning with *what, where* or *why* are rarely used. Instead, questions are deliberately shaped to offer only restricted responses, sometimes confined to mere *yes/no* responses.

Paul Simpson and Andrea Mayr (2010: 82) state that presupposition strategies are frequently used during interrogation and cross-examination. Presupposition assumes knowledge of what a response will be based on how a statement or question is phrased.

- Iteratives: e.g. 'Did you visit the crime scene *again*?' Again states that this is a repeated action. Here, the presupposition is that the defendant has already attended the crime scene. Phrasing the question as 'did you' allows only for a yes/no response, and therefore does not allow for the initial idea of 'visiting the crime scene' to be disputed.

- **Change of state verbs:** e.g. 'Did you *continue* to threaten my client?' This presupposes that the client was threatened by the person being interrogated; what is being asked here is if that threat was repeated, not if the *threat* actually happened.

- Factives: e.g. 'Do you *regret* entering the house that night?' This question seeks to clarify how the defendant feels about an action; a yes/no response does not allow for the defendant to deny actually entering the property.

- **Alternative questions:** e.g. 'Were you inside *or* outside the building on the night in question?' Although an optional question is provided, both options presuppose proximity to the building. The structure of the option question is limited to only one of two possible options: *inside* or *outside*.

- Cleft structures: e.g. '*It was you* who prompted the sick attack.' Phrasing this as a statement does not allow the defendant to respond, and does not allow the defendant to argue against whether or not the 'sick attack' took place. Stating 'it was you' at the start of the statement presupposes that the defendant is responsible for the 'sick attack'.

- **Comparators:** e.g. 'The co-accused seems to be *as short tempered as you*.' Agreement or denial does not challenge the presupposition that the defendant is 'short tempered'.

- **'Wh-type' questions:** e.g. '*Where* exactly did you put the stash?' This presupposes that the defendant was the agent; the question simply seeks to clarify location of 'the stash'.

- **Genitive constructions:** e.g. 'Where exactly did you put *your* stash?' The possessive determiner frames the defendant's ownership of 'the stash'.

- **Definite referring expressions:** e.g. 'Where exactly was *the* stash?' This presupposes that the defendant knows exactly what 'stash' is being referred to.

> **KEY TERMS**
>
> **Presupposition:** an implied precondition or assumption
>
> **Iterative:** a statement or expression that denotes repeated actions
>
> **Factive:** a verb that asserts the truth of a following clause
>
> **Cleft structure:** a sentence or clause that is split to form an additional, foregrounded clause using the structure *it + form of the verb be + focus + relative clause…*

All these techniques are designed to elicit a response that will help the lawyer build a stronger case, to either prove innocence or guilt.

A further strategy favoured by lawyers is to reformulate a response, allowing for clarification for the audience. However, a reformulation will not always use the exact phrasing that was initially used, and thus allows for the lawyer to present the statement in terms which will further the argument, as Text 7I shows.

Text 7I

Witness: I did not tell them everything.

Lawyer: [...] You did not tell them everything, did you, so you *concealed* certain things did you not?

Extract from Durant and Leung (2016)

Here, the lawyer reformulates the witness's use of the vague term 'everything'. The lexical choice of 'concealed' implies secrecy and underhand behaviour, which could be used against the witness to suggest that he or she is not reliable.

7 Language and Power

ACTIVITY 7.4
Question formulation and reformulation

Read Texts 7J–7M, which are all questions presented to Jeffrey Skilling during cross-examination at the Enron fraud trial. How are the questions formulated? What is the purpose of these questions? Are they all designed to elicit information or are some questions intended for other purposes?

Text 7J

Mr Skilling, you said in your testimony that you are somewhat of a business history buff. Can you think of a bigger mess in business than we have here with the Enron situation in recent history?

Text 7K

I want to tell you, if you look at Ms. Watkins testimony, she says it in a sentence. 'My understanding as an accountant,' she says, is that a company could never use its own stock to generate gain or avoid a loss on its income statement. Is that true? Were you aware of that?

Text 7L

Fitzgerald:	What was the Enron equity?
Skilling:	I don't know.
Fitzgerald:	You didn't know?
Skilling:	No.
Fitzgerald:	Did Enron put its own stock into the Raptors?
Skilling:	I believe if you go back to the board minutes where it was approved, that would have laid out in detail what the specific…
Fitzgerald:	You were aware Enron had issued its own stock to the Raptors, were you not?

Text 7M

> Now, Jordan Mintz, an Enron lawyer, testified that he tried to get you to sign approval sheets for the LJM deals and reminded you that your signature was required. I understand that you've said that you didn't believe your signature was required. Is that correct?

RESEARCH QUESTION

There are many examples of fictional courtroom proceedings, both in literature, such as *To Kill a Mockingbird*, or *The Crucible*, and as part of television dramas such as *The Good Wife*, or *Silk*. Examine an example of courtroom interaction, whether that is in opening and closing statements where the jury may be directly addressed, or in the cross-examination of witnesses, including expert witnesses. Consider patterns of legal language use in these texts. How closely do they reflect real courtroom proceedings?

You could compare a fictional account with the dramatisation of a real trial, such as *American Crime Story: The People v. OJ Simpson*, to see how closely the drama has reflected the trial.

Wider reading

Read more about the nature of power and legal language in the following books:

Conley, J.M. and O'Barr, W. (2005) *Just Words: Law, Language and Power*. (Second edition). London: University of Chicago Press.

Durant, A. and Leung, J.H.C. (2016) *Language and Law: A Resource Book for Students*. Abingdon: Routledge.

Mooney, A. (2014) *Language and Law*. London: Palgrave Macmillan.

Simpson, P. and Mayr, A. (2010) *Language and Power: A Resource Book for Students*. Abingdon: Routledge.

Ideas and answers

Chapter 1
Activity 1.1
You may have considered that titles:

- such as 'Miss' or 'Mrs' can take away a person's individuality
- can categorise people according to marital status
- can reinforce gender stereotypes and male dominance
- don't reflect modern society
- don't take into account transgender
- can be something to be proud of
- can rightfully reflect our position in society.

Activity 1.2
This is a subjective exercise, but your continuum might look something like this:

MOST EMOTIVE ⟶ LEAST EMOTIVE

Unsafe   appalling   insufficient   serious   very poor   limited privacy

Chapter 2
Activity 2.2
Other language features that create power are:

- the noun phrase 'high quality care'
- list of three: 'revalidation, appraisal and job planning processes'
- abstract nouns: e.g. 'compassion'
- semantic field: e.g. 'compliance', 'policy', 'procedures'
- use of the first-person subject pronoun 'I'
- verb choices: e.g. 'respecting', 'abide', 'bear'.

Ideas and answers

Activity 2.3
The following techniques are used to create a positive climate:

- modifiers such as 'nice' to describe the work being done
- modifiers such as 'excellent' to encourage and praise the students
- intensifiers + modifiers to encourage and praise: 'absolutely brilliant'
- direct address using the second-person pronoun 'you'
- use of students' first names
- use of personal terms of address such as 'darling'
- use of imperatives to encourage: 'go on'
- use of conditional rather than imperative to appear less direct: 'if you put the sheets…'
- use of interrogatives/modal auxiliaries rather than imperatives to appear less direct: 'can you get your orange books out…'
- informal lexical choices such as 'yeah', 'blew our minds', 'crack it'
- use of humour: 'excuses excuses excuses'
- use of the first-person plural pronoun 'we' to create a sense of inclusivity.

Activity 2.4
A key aspect of language and power is the different roles people have. This links to the concepts of hierarchy and status, and how, as a society, we accept certain roles. These roles can change depending on context.

In the first scenario, the son will adopt the role of student whilst the father will fulfil his role as teacher. There will be an accepted difference in status within the school environment. It is likely the son will behave like all other students towards his father. His language will likely reflect this, for example using 'sir', and follow politeness features common in teacher/student exchange. Similarly the father will use the features common to those in power.

In the second scenario, the son now has the status. However, it could be argued that given the more informal context of a football field, there won't be as significant a difference in language use between the two. For example, the father isn't likely to use a specific term of address towards the son. However, the son may show some power through, for example, the use of imperatives in telling his father (and the team) what to do.

Language and Power

Activity 2.5

You might have considered using positive politeness techniques:

- giving compliments

- listening to your parents

- using terms of address to reflect a close relationship.

Chapter 3

Activity 3.1

The impact of individual word choices is clear.

We have/They have: The connotation here is that the Iraqi army are focused on combat and conflict. The use of 'machine' takes away any sense of humanity; they are programmed to fight.

We/They: The difference in verb choices suggests that the British Army's actions are to protect rather than destroy lives, deliberately avoiding verbs such as 'kill'.

We launch/They launch: The connotation here is that the British Army is well prepared and efficient in protecting its troops.

Our boys are/Their boys are: The informal nouns used to describe the troops attempt to create sympathy for the British Army as the connotation is of young men risking their lives for their country. The modifiers create an image of heroic and courageous men in direct contrast to the Iraqi soldiers, whose patriotism is not considered.

Our missiles cause/Their missiles cause: The noun phrase 'collateral damage' avoids any reference to innocent people being killed.

Activity 3.2

You may get lost. But not in the crowd. The phrase 'not in the crowd' suggests that by driving a Porsche you will stand out.

Don't listen to anyone who says you can't have a Porsche. The use of the imperative 'don't listen' and the modal auxiliary 'can't' suggests a sense of defiance and that you can be different; you can have a Porsche.

Your mother would be proud. Your father, jealous. This suggests that the Porsche owner has done well in life and is in a better financial position than his father, reinforcing the idea of being part of an elite group.

Absolutely wrong for so, so many people. The connotation here is that whilst a Porsche might not be the ideal for the majority, it certainly is for the minority. By driving a Porsche you have some form of status, which doesn't make it 'absolutely wrong'.

Ideas and answers

Activity 3.3

You could group the language features as in this table:

• you can • your child • you won't see it	The pronoun choices will have an impact on the audience. The second person pronoun 'you' helps create a pseudo-relationship and tries to make the audience more empathetic to the situation.
• simply text • already has	The modifiers 'simply' and 'already' are likely to make the audience feel that they can make a difference because the solution to the problem is easily achievable.
• please don't wait	The use of a mitigated imperative adds an element of politeness to the advert to engage the audience.
• will kill • kill them • save a child's life	The repeated references throughout the advert to life and death will have an emotional impact on the audience.
• dirty water • clean water	The juxtaposition of 'dirty' with 'clean' is used twice to show what can happen if the audience supports the campaign.
• give WaterAid three pounds • give three pounds now	Repeating the amount requested emphasises the message: the audience is likely to feel that £3 is something they can afford.
• fourteen hundred • more than Malaria and AIDS combined • In the next minute	The use of facts and statistics is a common feature of influential power texts and will help the audience appreciate the scale of the problem.
• Children, child	Repeated references to children plays on the emotions, making the audience likely to respond to this tragedy.

Practice question

The key word is 'evaluate'; you can either agree or disagree with the statement, offering differing views and opinions including your own. You could begin by agreeing that language can be manipulative, covering the following points.

- Introduce the concept of 'audience positioning' and how 'dominant readings' are linked to the idea of manipulation.
- Give some specific examples of how language can influence our views, beliefs and opinions. First you could consider the language of journalists (with a reference to Shalini Singh), discussing aspects such as headlines, name

Language and Power

choices and referencing, and front covers. You could then discuss advertising, covering the different ways language is used to influence the receiver.

You could then present a counter-argument, in order to evaluate the statement. You could return to audience positioning and discuss how, on occasions, we do not accept what we read and see. You could also discuss the idea of impartiality and how language is not always used to manipulate how we see the world but to give us facts and information.

Chapter 4

Activity 4.1

You may have discussed:

- using language only used in your job
- using language you had never used before
- using language you didn't understand before
- using language that helped get your job done effectively
- using terms of address for different people depending on the hierarchy
- using politeness when talking to customers.

Activity 4.2

The precision helps avoid ambiguity and makes the difference in the offence very clear. This is achieved through the legal definitions which make a clear distinction between different offences. The phrase 'armed with a weapon' helps differentiate this offence from the more routine form of burglary.

You may have thought of the following points in relation to the second part of the activity:

- Many professions use jargon for precision but you may have discussed the following: doctors, surgeons, nurses, lawyers, solicitors, vets, police.
- The main benefit is to eradicate any potential mistakes. For example, a surgeon has to give very specific requests to those supporting in the operating theatre to avoid any confusion, as any mistakes would be catastrophic. Exclusive language also helps create an effective discourse community and a sense of loyalty amongst staff.

Practice question

You could discuss the following theories about language and power.

- Instrumental power – roles, hierarchy, status
- Power behind the discourse

Ideas and answers

- Politeness
- Face.

You should consider who actually has the power in this conversation. Does the customer because they have the right to cancel their membership? Or does the staff member because they have the company's authority to carry out the customer's requests? You may come to the conclusion that they both have power and show this in different ways. You could use the following examples to show the power of each person.

Staff member uses:

- Politeness
- Use of interrogatives to direct and control the conversation
- Terms of address
- Register
- Modifiers to try and persuade
- First-person pronoun
- Inclusive pronoun 'us'
- No hedges or other non-fluency features.

Customer uses:

- Negative responses to questions
- Politeness.

Chapter 5

Activity 5.1

You are likely to have found the following language features in the transcripts.

Text 5C

Interrogatives	Alright with that, Elle alright, so what do you think…, but why do you think that's important
Imperatives	Separate them…
Use of a student's name	Elle, Ryan

Language and Power

Discourse markers	So, right
IRF discourse structure	T: so what do you think might be at the top P1: erm (.) I was thinking when it were written T: yes when it was written that's definitely important
Revoicing	P1: erm (.) I was thinking when it were written T: yes when it was written that's definitely important (.) P2: could audience be up there T: audience (.) yes I think it would up there
Wait time	any other ideas (2) Ryan

Text 5D

Interrogatives	Who can remember…, how can we make sure…, what's the test…, what does that test for, are you listening Jack
Imperatives	Let's get settled, let's all think…, have a try
Use of a student's name	Michael, Zoe, James, Jack Nicola, Anne
Politeness markers	Thank you, well done for having a go
Discourse markers	Okay
IRF discourse structure	T: what's the test for carbon dioxide (2) Michael P1: a glowing splint T: a glowing splint no that's not the one
Revoicing	P1: a glowing splint T: a glowing splint no that's not the one P2: hydrogen T: not hydrogen (3) not hydrogen no P3: oxygen T: oxygen (.) what does it do to it Nicola P3: relights the splint T: relights the splint (.)
Wait time	not hydrogen (3) not hydrogen no…

Ideas and answers

The teacher might have used these language features for the following purposes.

- **Interrogatives:** To involve students in the lesson; check knowledge; clarify understanding; make students think; extend students' answers to develop their knowledge and understanding; ensure students aren't passive in the classroom.
- **Imperatives:** To give clear instructions; encourage students.
- **Students' names:** To help create relationships; directly involve certain students, ensuring all are listening.
- **Politeness markers:** To praise and encourage students; model politeness.
- **Discourse markers:** To gain attention; signify a change in focus.
- **IRF discourse structure:** To consolidate learning; eradicate any misunderstanding; involve others in the discussion.
- **Revoicing:** To draw other students' attention to a comment and show its importance; encourage better understanding, further discussion and contribution.
- **Wait time:** To encourage further discussion and contribution; allow students time to think.

Activity 5.2

There is a clear dominance by the teacher and an apparent reluctance to let the students contribute. The teacher dominates by holding the floor and not giving many turn-yielding cues. Even when the teacher asks questions they do not give any wait time and instead continue talking. The opportunities for effective IRF are missed.

The teacher could do the following to facilitate a more collaborative classroom:

- Offer reflective comments.
- Invite students to respond by being more direct (e.g. using their name).
- Say nothing and use silence as a tool to encourage discussion: use wait time.
- Act as more of a facilitator rather than just giving constant instructions.

Chapter 6
Activity 6.1
Text 6B
- The noun phrase 'The Tories' is used rather than the more formal 'Conservative Party', undermining their status and prestige.

Language and Power

- 'The Tories' are the agents of the sentence – they are presented as actively responsible for 'holding Britain back'.
- The metaphor 'holding Britain back' is illustrated in a literal way, with the graphology of a hand physically tugging at the country.
- The hand pulling back Britain is wearing a blue bangle. Blue represents the colour of the Conservative Party, in marked contrast with the red of the Labour party.
- The bangle suggests that the current leader of the Conservative Party, a woman, is personally responsible for holding the country back.
- The present perfect verb choice 'have held' suggests the prolonged duration of negative Tory influence on Britain's progress, an influence which continues to present time.
- The adverbial 'long enough' emphasises the need for change – the situation cannot be allowed to continue.
- 'Time to build' is elliptical, omitting 'it is'. This creates an emphatic and direct tone, one which reflects how the Labour Party is presenting itself – they are the party who will 'build', not 'hold back'.
- The logo 'For the many not the few' is repeated, emphasising the Labour Party's goal – fair government for all rather than just the privileged.

Text 6C

- The image assumes a shared understanding – the audience is expected to know who the person is and her association with Scotland.
- A homophonic pun is used: adding the silent *b* to 'referendum' foregrounds the message of the text, that to hold a referendum is not the smart thing to do.
- The pun is anchored in the main body of the text 'it'd be <u>stupid</u>', reinforcing the message.
- Repetition of the determiner 'more' with negative nouns suggests persistence: 'More instability'; 'More uncertainty'.
- The persistence is reinforced with the determiner *another* and the adverb 'now'.
- The contracted form 'it'd' adds a level of informality but also certainty to the declarative, with the modal verb 'would' suggesting terrible consequences from a referendum.
- 'scotlandinunion' appears without conventional word spacing, reinforcing the message presented with the imperative 'join us'.
- The image of a thistle, Scotland's national flower, underlines pride in Scottish identity.

Ideas and answers

Activity 6.2

Ethos

Obama uses first-person pronouns throughout. He aligns himself with the country and the public by using plural pronouns 'we' and 'us', but also speaks personally, of his own opinions and beliefs. This is most emphasised in 'I'm not on the ballot again'. 'I'm not looking to score some points', reinforcing that his argument is for the benefit of others, not himself.

His authoritative stance is reinforced in the penultimate paragraph: 'I believe in the Second Amendment… I taught constitutional law'. He underscores his status as someone with the expertise to comment on these very important issues. However, this is not self-aggrandisement: 'I know a little about this'. The modifier 'little' presents him as humble too.

In Paragraph 2 Obama identifies the issue of gun control measures as a 'problem', and considers what his 'goal' is. Thus, Obama presents himself as someone who is able to solve this problem, and he proposes to act, rather than simply to engage in debate. Thus, he presents himself as a man of action.

Pathos

Obama stirs up public reaction by using heightened, emotive language to remind the audience why gun control measures are necessary – they destroy lives:

- 'violence' is a main theme throughout, reinforced by 'gun violence' and 'mass violence'
- ideas about life and death are presented: 'people are dying'; 'save lives'.

Explicit reference is made to America: 'advanced country'; 'a civilized society', creating a sense of pride, but also dismay at the violence such a society is engaged in.

Reference to Dr King creates a link between civil rights and gun violence, reinforcing the need for urgent action to prevent more loss of life, as before in America's history.

Reference to 'a little boy like Daniel' uses direct naming, creating a personal identity. The adjective *little* is associated with innocence.

There is a proliferation of positive mental verbs: 'care'; 'believe'; 'cherish', indicating Obama's confidence that his audience shares his beliefs and ideology.

Logos

Obama presents a carefully structured, reasoned argument.

- He outlines the problem at the outset. It is not only gun violence, but the public's lack of action to prevent further acts of violence as they have 'become numb' and think this is 'normal'.

Language and Power

- He moves from 'thinking' and ' debates' to 'do something to try to prevent the next [shooting]'. Words alone are no longer enough – action is needed.
- Balanced phrasing reinforces his message that gun control can exist alongside the Second Amendment: e.g. 'We all believe in the First Amendment… but we accept that you can't yell "fire" in a theater'. He begins with an accepted principle, then illustrates how, in reality, there are associated conditions which the public also accepts.

Activity 6.3

All three texts make use of concrete references to describe abstract concepts.

Text 6G

'A fiery stream' gives a very visual image of verbal rage, perhaps calling forth an image of the fires of hell. This 'fiery stream' is linked to 'biting ridicule' and 'blasting reproach' in which the adjectives reflect material verbs, creating a sense of physical outpouring. The metonym 'nation's ear' represents the consciousness and awareness of the American people; hearing Douglass' words will alter their very beliefs and ideas.

Text 6H

'The energy, the faith, the devotion' – can all be 'seen' more clearly when associated with 'light', which helps us find our way through difficult times, and is often associated with religious devotion and hope in times of darkness and hardship.

Text 6I

'The American dream' is an ideal, a hope that our aspirations and goals can be achieved. Linking this abstract 'ideal' to a race suggests that it is something that can be 'won'. Castro likens the 'Dream' to a variety of races: 'sprint'; 'marathon'; 'relay' to suggest the different ways that the 'Dream' can be realised, through endurance, and by working as a team.

Activity 6.4

Questioning techniques

KG-M uses a variety of question types to direct the structure of the interview.

- Optional question eliciting one of two responses: 'Were you at work on Monday or were you out campaigning' allows him to build on DD's response to imply criticism of his actions.
- Tag questions: 'this election … has been a huge distraction <u>hasn't it</u>' presses DD to confirm KG-M's own stance about the timing of the election.

- Closed question: 'in March you admitted that you hadn't costed the economic impact of no deal ... <u>have you done one yet</u>' elicits a single response, which can then be explored more fully.

Face and politeness

DD attempts to maintain politeness by using a formal address term: 'Mr Guru–Murthy'. However, both speakers directly challenge positive face.

KG-M uses:

- second-person pronouns to direct statements at DD, e.g. 'this election has been a huge distraction to <u>your</u> job'.
- generic pronoun 'you' to challenge DD's actions: e.g. 'you'd have thought that you as the Brexit secretary (.) were sitting down to have a look at them...' implies that DD ought to have been 'sitting down to have a look'.
- explicit reference to DD's role: e.g. 'this election has been a huge distraction to your job' implies that he is failing to meet the job's requirements.
- noun phrases: e.g. 'two big documents'; 'a huge distraction' to emphasise the scale of the work he implies DD is not prioritising.
- the verb 'admitted', which implies that DD's statement was a confession of wrong-doing.

DD uses:

- a face-saving technique when he attempts to challenge KG-M's implication that he cannot read documents on the campaign trail: 'it's the wonders of modern technology ... that you can actually er read things on ipads on the train' suggests multiple tasks can be accomplished without any of them suffering.
- face-threat of a participant not involved in the discussion. 'I don't need to read them in the studio like Mr Corbyn' implies DD is fully equipped to deal with issues, whilst the opposition, Mr Corbyn, is not.
- face-threatening behaviour when addressing KG-M directly: 'would you like the answer' implies the interviewer's role is to listen to responses as well as pose questions.
- face-threat when he addresses KG-M's point about costing the EU exit: you're summarising something let me tell you what it is' establishes DD as authoritative, implying that KG-M's 'summary' has fallen short and DD can explain more fully.

Cooperative speech

There is clear turn-taking, with appropriate use of adjacency pairs. However, there is also evidence of simultaneous speech as both speakers struggle to hold the floor.

Language and Power

DD fails to abide by the maxim of quantity: his responses to KG-M's questions are lengthy and begin to obscure the focus. Much of his response focuses on Theresa May, not on the actual question: DD's own preparedness for the Brexit negotiation.

Manner is not fully abided by when DD attempts to comment on present events (the British election) and future events (the Brexit negotiations). He shifts from present tense ('one of the points of this election is to reinforce') to projection of the future ('she'll have a mandate'), whilst recognising that Theresa May's position is not a certainty ('if she's elected'). This makes his response to the question unclear.

DD also flouts relevance in his reference to Mr Corbyn, not responding to the question but redirecting focus to an opponent's lack of technological proficiency.

Chapter 7

Activity 7.1

Legislative documents: The Press Commission Code of Conduct; Consumer Protection Act

Private law documents: Last will and testament; music copyright licence; rental tenancy agreement

Procedural documents: Document providing details to a jury about codes of behaviour

Activity 7.2

The language features include:

- use of first-person plural pronouns, to speak on behalf of the organisation
- use of second-person pronouns to speak directly to the audience: 'what to do if you've got any concerns'; 'you may be entitled to … a refund'
- use of deontic modal verbs to indicate force (e.g 'we will', 'we shall') and epistemic modal verbs (e.g. 'we might') to indicate options available to consumers
- use of conditional clauses (e.g. 'if we have a belief in the good faith…'), which allow for different circumstances and scenarios
- listing (e.g. 'companies, organisations or individuals'; 'people's safety and rights')
- an accessible register, so that rules are clearly understood
- contractions to lower the register (e.g. 'That's why we have a few rules')
- a more formal register to convey authority (e.g. 'ensure compliance')
- reference to a shared ideology (e.g. 'We want our services to help customers')

Ideas and answers

- vague language (e.g. 'take appropriate action'), which does not commit the organisation to any particular course of action
- mitigation (e.g. 'we have a few rules'), which lessens the impact
- explicit reference to non-compliance (e.g. 'a few rules … if you break them')
- use of a direct threat (e.g. 'we will contact the police').

Activity 7.3

Attempts to convince the audience of Lay and Skilling's guilt include the following:

- Repetition of words linked to the semantic field of dishonesty (e.g. 'lies'; 'mislead'; 'the true financial condition')
- Emphasis on the success of the defendants (e.g. 'as fortunate as these two men')
- Emphasis on their culpability (e.g. 'two men at the helm of the company')
- Use of verbs are associated with the defendants to suggest they were agents of the fraud and wholly responsible (e.g. 'knew'; 'worked to lie and to mislead'; 'violated').

Ways the victims are presented include the following:

- Explicitly referenced as 'the common investors'; 'the investing public'; 'employees', suggesting the wide range of victims
- Emphasis on victims' lack of information (e.g. 'deprived … of information')
- The victims are presented as the target for the action (e.g. 'lies that deprived the common investors'), suggesting their powerlessness
- The victims are presented as disadvantaged in comparison with the defendants: 'the victims in this case … were not as fortunate as these two men'.

Activity 7.4
Text 7J

Invites a yes/no response, but either response would condemn the defendant. Either response presupposes that this is indeed a 'big mess'.

Text 7K

The use of two questions makes it difficult to know which to address first. An affirmative response could refer to whether or not:

- a company should use its own stock to generate gain
- the defendant was aware of the principle of not using a company's own stock

- the defendant was aware of Ms. Watkins' testimony
- Ms. Watkins' testimony is correct.

Text 7L

Repetition of Skilling's response as a question suggests disbelief: 'You didn't know?'

The cleft structure presents a declarative, 'You were aware Enron had issued its own stock to the Raptors', suggesting that this is a fact. The question tagged to the end 'were you not?' allows only for a yes/no response, but neither would allow the presupposition that Enron issued its own stock to be disputed. It only allows Skilling to comment on his own level of awareness.

Text 7M

The polar question 'is that correct?' allows only for a yes/no response. However, it follows two lengthy declaratives: 'an Enron lawyer testified … approval sheets' and 'I understand … was required'. It is unclear which point the question addresses. Is the Enron lawyer's testimony correct? Or are Skilling's own words about his signature correctly represented here?

Transcription key

(.)	indicates a pause of less than a second
(2)	indicates a longer pause (number of seconds indicated)
Bold	indicates stressed syllables or words
: :	indicates elongation of a word
((*italics*))	indicates contextual or additional information
[ ]	indicates the start and end points of simultaneous speech

References

Amnesty International (2017) 'Urgent action: refugees at great risk due to unsafe camps'. Available at: www.amnesty.org/download/Documents/EUR2560912017ENGLISH.pdf.

Althusser, L. (1970) 'Ideology and ideological state apparatuses', *La Pensée*. Available at: www.marxists.org/reference/archive/althusser/1970/ideology.htm (trans. B. Brewster).

Arrieta-Kenna, R. (2016) 'These are the only 6 newspapers in the country to endorse Donald Trump', *Politico Magazine*. Available at: www.politico.com/magazine/story/2016/10/donald-trump-newspaper-endorsements-214390.

Bas-Wohlert, C. (2012) 'Swedish needs a gender-neutral pronoun', *The Local*, 8 February. Available at: www.thelocal.se/20120208/38992.

Bernstein, B. (1960) 'Language and social class'. *British Journal of Sociology*, 11 (3): 271–276.

Brown, P. and Levinson, S. (1987) *Politeness: Some Universals in Language Usage*. Cambridge: Cambridge University Press.

Cameron-Faulkner, T., Lieven, E. and Tomasello, M. (2003) 'A construction-based analysis of child directed speech', *Cognitive Science*, 27 (6).

Chilton, P. (2004). *Analysing Political Discourse: Theory and Practice*. London: Routledge.

Chilton, P. and Shäffner, C. (2002) *Politics as Text and Talk: Analytic Approaches to Political Discourse*. Amsterdam: John Benjamins Publishing Company.

Crystal, D. (2010). In A. Durant and J.H.C. Leung (2016) *Language and Law*. Abingdon: Routledge (English Language Introductions).

Dillon, J.T. (1983). In C.B. Cazden (1988) *Classroom Discourse: Teaching and the art of questioning*. Phi Delta Kappa Educational Foundation

Durant, A. and Leung, J.H.C (2016) *Language and Law*. Abingdon: Routledge (English Language Introductions).

Eckert, P. (2006) 'Communities of Practice'. In K. Brown (ed.) *Encyclopedia of Language and Linguistics* (Second edition). Amsterdam: Elsevier, 683.

Elliott, L. (2017) 'World's eight richest people have same wealth as poorest 50%', *The Guardian*. Available at: www.theguardian.com/global-development/2017/jan/16/worlds-eight-richest-people-have-same-wealth-as-poorest-50.

Equality and Human Rights Commission (2016) 'Race report: Healing a divided Britain'. Available at: www.equalityhumanrights.com/en/race-report-healing-divided-britain.

Fairclough, N. (2014) *Language and Power*. Harlow: Pearson Education.

References

Fairclough, N. (1992) Critical Discourse Analysis: The Critical Study of Language. London: Routledge. Diagram adapted from B. Paltridge (2006) *Discourse Analysis: An introduction.* London: Continuum International.

Fairclough, N. and Wodak, R. (1997) 'Critical Discourse Analysis'. In T.A. van Dijk (1997) *Discourse as Social Interaction.* London: Sage, pp: 258–284

Field, J. (2004) *Psycholinguistics: The Key Concepts.* London: Routledge.

Friginal, E. (2009) *The Language of Outsourced Call Centers: A Corpus-Based Study of Cross-Cultural Interaction.* Philadelphia, PA: John Benjamins Publishing.

Goffman, E. (1967) 'On face work: an analysis of ritual elements of social interaction'. In E. Goffman (1967) *Interaction Ritual: Essays in Face-to-Face Behaviour.* Chicago: Aldine Transaction.

Grice, P. (1975) 'Logic and conversation'. In A. Jaworski and N. Coupland (eds) (1999) *The Discourse Reader.* Abingdon: Routledge.

Guy, G.R. (1988) 'Language and social class'. In F.J. Newmeyer (ed.) (1988) *Linguistics: The Cambridge Survey (Volume 4, Language: The Social-Cultural Context).* Cambridge: Cambridge University Press, 37.

Hall, S. (1973) *Encoding and Decoding in the Television Discourse.* University of Birmingham: Centre for Cultural Studies.

Hall, S., Hobson, D., Love, A. and Willis, P. (eds) (1980) *Culture, Media, Language.* London: Hutchinson.

Holmes, J. (2006) *Gendered Talk at Work.* London, Blackwell.

Holmes, J. (2009a) 'Discourse in the workplace literature review' (*Language in the Workplace Occasional Papers Number 12*). Wellington: Victoria University of Wellington. Available at: www.victoria.ac.nz/lals/centres-and-institutes/language-in-the-workplace/docs/ops/OP-12.pdf.

Holmes, J. (2009b). 'Meeting talk: an introduction', *Journal of Business Communication*, 46 (1): 3–22.

Holmes, J. and Stubbe, M. (2003) *Power and Politeness in the Workplace: A Sociolinguistic Analysis of Talk at Work.* Abingdon: Routledge.

Jesperson, O. (1922) *Language: Its Nature, Development and Origin.* London: George Allen & Unwin.

Kollataj, A. (2009) 'Jargon and Colloquialisms' The Cyprus journal of sciences, Vol 7. Available at: http://linguistics.stackexchange.com/questions/3973/why-is-jargon-sometimes-used-instead-of-familiar-words.

Kraus, M.W. and Keltner, D. (2009). 'Signs of socioeconomic status: a thin-slicing approach', *Psychological Science,* 20 (1), pp.99–106.

Lave, J. and Wenger, E. (1991) *Situated Learning: Legitimate Peripheral Participation.* Cambridge: Cambridge University Press.

Lemke, J. (1982). In C.B. Cazden (1988) *Classroom Discourse: The Language of Teaching and Learning.* London: Heinemann.

Lukes, S. (1974). *Power: A Radical View* (Second edition 2005). Basingstoke: Palgrave Macmillan.

Moore, R.B. (1976). *Racism in the English language: a lesson plan and study essay.* Utica, NY: Racism and Sexism Resource Center for Educators.

Obama, M. (2016). 'Let girls learn' event speech. Madrid: Spain. Available at: https://obamawhitehouse.archives.gov/the-press-office/2016/06/30/remarks-first-lady-let-girls-learn-event-madrid-spain

O'Connor, M.C. and Michaels, S. (1996) 'Shifting participant frameworks: orchestrating thinking practises in group discussions'. In D. Hicks (ed.) *Discourse, Learning, and Schooling*. Cambridge: Cambridge University Press, pp: 63–103.

Office for National Statistics (2016). Available at: www.ons.gov.uk/peoplepopulationandcommunity/householdcharacteristics/homeinternetandsocialmediausage/bulletins/internetaccesshouseholdsandindividuals/2016.

Orwell, G. (1945) *Politics and the English Language*. London. Penguin Books.

Richardson, J.E. (2006). *Analysing Newspapers: An Approach from Critical Discourse Analysis*. London: Palgrave Macmillan.

Ringler, N.M. (1981) 'The development of language and how adults talk to children', *Infant Mental Health Journal*, 2 (2): pp. 71–83.

Romaine, S. (1999) *Communicating Gender*. Mahwah, N.J.: L. Erlbaum Associates.

Rowe, M.B. (1986) 'Wait time: slowing down may be a way of speeding up!', *Journal of Teacher Education*, 37 (43–48).

Schumer, S. (2014) *The Language of Parenting: A Parenting Guide Designed to Help Parents Meet the Everyday Challenges of Parenting!* Dartford: Xlibris.

Simpson, P. and Mayr, A. (2010) *Language and Power: A Resource Book for Students*. Abingdon: Routledge.

Sinclair, J. and Coulthard, M. (1975). *Towards an Analysis of Discourse*. Oxford: Oxford University Press.

Singh, S. (2016) 'Mass communication or mass manipulation? Is journalism living up to the ideals it espouses?', 17 February. Available at: www.newslaundry.com/2016/02/17/mass-communication-or-mass-manipulation-is-journalism-living-up-to-the-ideals-it-espouses.

Spolsky, B. (1998) *Sociolinguistics*. Oxford: OUP.

Thomas, L. and Wareing, (2004) *Language, Society and Power: An Introduction* (Second Edition). London: Routledge.

Tiersma, P. (1999) 'The Nature of Legal Language'. Available at: www.languageandlaw.org.

Trudgill, P. (2000) *Sociolinguistics: An Introduction to Language and Society*. London: Penguin.

UNDP (2015) 'Gender Inequality Index (GII)', *Human Development Report*. Available at: http://hdr.undp.org/en/content/gender-inequality-index-gii.

van Dijk, T.A. (2008) *Discourse and Power*. Basingstoke: Palgrave Macmillan.

Wenger, E. (2000) *Communities of Practice: Learning, Meaning, and Identity*. Cambridge: Cambridge University Press.

World Bank (2012) 'Dollar benchmark: the rise of the $1-a-day statistic'. Available at: www.bbc.co.uk/news/magazine-17312819.

Young, W. (2013) 'Using the word "gay" to mean "crap" is a form of bullying of gay people'. *The Guardian*, 24 November.

Glossary

accent: variation in pronunciation associated with a particular geographical region

adjacency pair: a simple structure of two turns

anaphora: the use of a word referring back to a word used earlier in a text to avoid repetition

archaic: an older word or style of language no longer in everyday use

audience positioning: the assumptions made in a text about its readers' background knowledge and understanding, attitudes and values in order to guide them towards an interpretation

binomial: two-part pairs or phrases, with words linked by the conjunction *and*

cleft structure: a sentence or clause that is split to form an additional, foregrounded clause using the structure *it + form of the verb be + focus + relative clause*....

converge: move language styles and patterns to more closely match those of other speakers

Critical Discourse Analysis (CDA): an approach to the study of written and spoken language focusing on the ways that power is enacted

dialect: variation in words and structures associated with a particular geographical region

discourse community: a group of people with shared interests and belief systems who are likely to respond to texts in similar ways

discourse marker: a word, phrase or clause that helps to organise what is said or written (e.g. 'OK', 'so', 'as I was saying…')

euphemisms: words or phrases that are substituted for more direct words or phrases in an attempt to make things easier to accept or less embarrassing

face-threatening act: a speech act that has the potential to damage someone's self-esteem

face-work: Goffman's term for the behaviours used in presenting or protecting our face to others, as well as those that show our respect of other speakers' 'faces'

factive: a verb that asserts the truth of a following clause

genre: a way of grouping texts based on expected shared conventions

hedges: words or phrases which soften what is said or written to make it less direct

holding the conversational floor: speaking until the speaker finished what they wish to say or until someone interrupts them

implicature: an implied meaning that has to be inferred by a speaker as a result of one of the maxims being broken

Language and Power

influential power: a type of power that is persuasive rather than imposing

in-group: an exclusive group of people with shared interests or identity.

initiation, response, evaluation/ feedback (IRE/IRF): three-part conversational exchange in which a speaker starts the conversation, a second speaker responds and the first speaker then provides some feedback to what the second speaker said

instrumental power: a type of power that is explicit and often imposed by a higher authority

iterative: a statement or expression that denotes repeated actions

jargon: the vocabulary and manner of speech that define and reflect a particular profession but are difficult for others to understand

kenning: a two-word compound expression, often providing a metaphorical meaning to an object or entity

legalese: the formal, technical language of legal documents, sometimes considered deliberately alienating for those not working within the legal profession

lexicon: the words used in a language or by a person or group of people

power asymmetry: a power imbalance between speakers shown by the unequal way they address each other

presupposition: an implied precondition or assumption

rhetoric: the art of persuasion or the means by which language is manipulated in order to persuade an audience

sociolect: the language used by a particular social group, e.g. teenage school children, adults in a book club

synthetic personalisation: making it seem as if text receivers are being addressed as individuals rather than as a mass

turn-yielding cue: when a speaker invites and encourages others in a conversation to respond, thus relinquishing control; this can be through pausing, intonation or lexical cues such as 'I think' and 'you know'

unequal encounters: when one speaker has accepted dominance over another influencing language choices

weasel words: words or statements that are intentionally ambiguous or misleading (in folklore, weasels are often untrustworthy, easily adapting to situations in order to manipulate others)

Index

Page numbers in italics are figures; with 't' are tables.

acronyms 52–3
advertising 40–8, 45t
audience positioning 32, 38, 41–2, 44–5

charity appeals 48
class inequality 5–6
codes 55
cohesion, in rhetoric 87
collaboration in education 71–4, *72*
complimenting consumers 41–2
conversational maxims 91
courtroom language 107–13
Critical Discourse Analysis (CDA) 11–12, *12*, 21, 76–83
customers/clients 60–2

discourse
  communities 53, 55
  power behind/in 15–19
  traditional classroom 65–71, *69*
  see also legal language; rhetoric

education 65–74, *69*, *72*
elite consumers, and advertising 42
emotion 7–8, 48–9
exclusive language 55–6

face/face-work 24–6, 90–1

gender, and inequality 2–3
genre 26, 27–8t

headlines 35–7, 37t

ideology, and politics 76–83
impartial reporting 40
inequality 2–6
influential power 14–15
instrumental power 12–13, 65–71, *69*
interviews, political 88–93, 89–90t
IRE/IRF (Initiation, Response, Evaluation/Feedback) 68, *69*

jargon 54–5
journalism 32–40, 33–4t, 37t, *39*

legal language 99–100
  in the courtroom 107–13
  written discourse 101–7

manifestos, political 80–3
manipulation 33–9, 33–4t, 37t
markers, discourse 66, 67
media 31–2, *31*
  journalism 32–40, 33–4t, 37t, *39*
meetings, in the workplace 56–9
metaphors, and rhetoric 86–7

naming, and journalism 37–9

occupational language 52–62
  see also legal language

parallelism, and rhetoric 87
parliamentary debate 93–7
patriotism, in advertising 43–5, 45t
personal power 19, 20–1
politeness 24–6, 90–1
politics 19–20
  and CDA 76–83
  and rhetoric 83–97, 89–90t
positive power 23–4
posters, political 76–80
'power over' 23
powerful language 22–3
pronouns, and rhetoric 85

racial inequality 5
referencing, and journalism 37–9
rhetoric, and politics 83–97, 89–90t

shock, in advertising 46–7
social groups 7, 19–20, 21–2
speech, power in 26t, 28t
speeches, political *see* rhetoric
synthetic personalisation 81–2

three-part lists, and rhetoric 88

weasel words 47–8
workplace interactions 56–60
writing 26t, 28t
  and legal discourse 101–7

Acknowledgements

The authors and publishers acknowledge the following sources of copyright material and are grateful for the permissions granted. While every effort has been made, it has not always been possible to identify the sources of all the material used, or to trace all copyright holders. If any omissions are brought to our notice, we will be happy to include the appropriate acknowledgements on reprinting.

Text 1A by permission of Amnesty International; Text 2A by permission of Monarch; Text 2B Department of Education © Crown Copyright; Text 2F Top firms reject candidates with 'working class accents' By Margaret Taylor, December 2010, www.thelawyer.com; Text 3A front cover of The Sun, 8 May 2015, by permission of News Corp; Text 3B front cover of the Daily Mirror 8 May 2015 by permission of Mirrorpix; Text 3C Image courtesy of The Advertising Archives; Text 3D Universal History Archive/Getty Images; Text 3E Hulton Archive/Getty Images; Text 3F Contraband Collection/Alamy Stock Photo; Text 3G photo by Achin Lippoth, poster used by permission of Innocence in Danger Germany; Text 6A The Conservative Party Archive/Getty Images; Text 6B Carl Court/Getty Images; Text 6C WENN Ltd/Alamy Stock Photo; Text 6D Plaid Cymru – The Party of Wales; Text 6E The American Presidency Project; Text 6M Hansard © Parliamentary Copyright

Development of this publication has made use of the Cambridge English Corpus (CEC). The CEC is a multi-billion word computer database of contemporary spoken and written English. It includes British English, American English and other varieties of English. It also includes the Cambridge Learner Corpus, developed in collaboration with Cambridge English Language Assessment. Cambridge University Press has built up the CEC to provide evidence about language use that helps to produce better language teaching materials.

Thanks to the following for permission to reproduce images:

Cover image: Ken Reid/Getty Images; Chapter opener images 1-7 iDJ Photography/Getty Images, Martin Barraud/Getty Images, Caiaimage/Tom Merton/Getty Images, Thomas Barwick/Getty Images, Hero Images/Getty Images, Nikhil Jayant/EyeEm/Getty Images, Peter Glass/Getty Images; Fig. 3.2 EnVogue_Photo/Alamy Stock Photo; Fig. 5.2 Hero Images/Getty Images

The publisher would like to thank the following members of The Cambridge Panel: English who assisted in reviewing this book: Pramod Kanakath, Sophie Collins, Khushnuma Gandhi.